In the United States, drug companies promoting their products to physicians are required by law to limit their claims to what they can prove, and to make full disclosure of all known hazards. Dr. Silverman, who is a noted science writer and pharmacologist, finds that many multinational drug companies are circumventing similar laws in Latin America in order to sell more of their products.

The author provides detailed comparisons of the promotion of 28 separate prescription drugs in the U.S. and in Mexico, Central America, Colombia, Ecuador, Brazil and other Latin American countries. Typically, claims for effectiveness are exaggerated in Latin America and the hazards are glossed over. This practice, denounced by Latin American medical experts and appalling even to scientists within the drug industry, is blamed for needless patient injury and death.

Evidence for the author's findings is contained mainly in the five standard pharmaceutical reference works in use in Latin America, which reprint information provided by drug companies, and the equivalent volume used by physicians in the U.S. The author also analyzes the context of law and practice in each of the countries examined.

Milton Silverman, Ph.D., is the co-author of *Pills, Profits, and Politics* (California, 1974) and is a member of the faculty of the University of California School of Pharmacy, San Francisco.

S0-BFH-687

THE DRUGGING
OF THE AMERICAS

131034

RM
301
,S53

THE DRUGGING
OF THE AMERICAS

How Multinational Drug Companies Say
One Thing about Their Products to
Physicians in the United States, and
Another Thing to Physicians in
Latin America

by
Milton Silverman

UNIVERSITY OF CALIFORNIA PRESS
BERKELEY • LOS ANGELES • LONDON

GOSHEN COLLEGE LIBRARY
GOSHEN, INDIANA

University of California Press
Berkeley and Los Angeles, California

University of California Press, Ltd.
London, England

Copyright © 1976 by Milton Silverman

ISBN 0-520-03122-9
Library of Congress Catalog Card Number: 75-27935
Printed in the United States of America

To the memory of

James Watkins — born 1942 — treated with chloramphenicol by a urologist and another physician, his own father, for a urinary tract infection — died 1952 in La Canada, California, from aplastic anemia.

Mary Patricia Corcoran — born 1947 — treated with chloramphenicol for a few days for a urinary tract infection — died 1952 in Evansville, Indiana, from aplastic anemia.

Brenda Lynne Elfstrom — born 1940 — treated with chloramphenicol for a sore throat and later for a minor urinary infection — died 1960 in Orange, California, from aplastic anemia.

Luisa A. — born 1915 — treated for six weeks with prednisone for arthritis — died 1970 in Guadalajara, Mexico, from fulminating tuberculosis.

Anna Maria P. — born 1931 — treated for five weeks with phenylbutazone for "severe shoulder pain" — died 1971 in Cali, Colombia, from agranulocytosis.

Agostino E. — born 1940 — treated with imipramine plus phenelzine for depression — died 1972 in Guayaquil, Ecuador, from hypertensive crisis.

Tomás R. — born 1966 — treated with chloramphenicol for tonsillitis — died 1973 in Mexico City from aplastic anemia.

Eleanor Roosevelt — born 1884 — treated for months with steroid hormones for anemia — died 1962 in New York City from reactivated tuberculosis.

And others. Many others.

CONTENTS

TABLES

EXPLANATION OF TABLES

Tables 1 to 20 were prepared from the verbatim translations of material taken from the 1973 editions of these books:

USA—*Physicians' Desk Reference*

MEXICO—*Diccionario de Especialidades Farmacéuticas, Edición Mexicana*

CENTRAL AMERICA and DOMINICAN REPUBLIC—*Ibid., Edición C.A.D.*

ECUADOR and COLOMBIA—*Ibid., Edición E. Co.*

BRAZIL—*Index Terapêutico Moderno*

ARGENTINA—*Therapia Vademecum*

(Note: Except for Argentina, the descriptive material in these books comes from the pharmaceutical companies. In Argentina, the companies have no responsibility for the published statements.)

In each instance, a check mark shows that the indication for use, contraindication and warning, or adverse reaction is included in the drug description for the countries concerned. Special note is made where no hazards are disclosed in the description.

The promotional material considered here may or may not be the same as that included in package inserts, miscellaneous company literature, or information presented orally by detail men. The 1973 descriptions do not necessarily correspond to statements made in 1975.

PREFACE

In the thirty-five years since I first visited and worked in Mexico, Central America, and South America as both a newspaperman and a scientist, many Latin Americans have honored me with not only their technical cooperation but also their warm friendship. I have come to understand the deep significance of the expression *mi casa es su casa.*

My house has been their house. More important, their house has been mine. And now I have learned that, beyond any question, their house is being despoiled by the great multinational drug companies. In the promotion of drugs to Latin American physicians, the values of these products have been grossly exaggerated and their hazards glossed over or totally ignored.

The companies involved are not only those based in the United States. Some have their headquarters in Western Europe. When called upon to explain the inconsistences in their promotional campaigns, their standard defense is "we're not breaking any laws." But in some Latin American countries, some of these global companies *have* been breaking laws. They have been lying.

The companies whose products are considered in this report are not the only offenders. Other firms, both international and domestic, have been performing in a similar fashion.

When the so-called morals of the marketplace are applied to drugs that can be invaluable when used properly, the result is not only the prostitution of science. It also means that physicians and pharmacists are uninformed or misinformed. Moreover, it means that patients are needlessly harmed.

Some of my scientific colleagues in the drug industry are already aware of the double standard of drug advertising—full disclosure in the United States, less than complete disclosure in the developing countries—and are appalled by it. Few seem to have known that the failure to reveal hazards to all physicians may represent a violation of national laws.

There is yet another aspect. In the United States, the major pharmaceutical companies have long and vociferously assailed the laws which now require them to restrict claims of efficacy of their products to those they can support with substantial scientific evidence and to inform physicians fully of all hazards. These rules, the companies have argued, are excessively harsh. They represent an interference in the sanctified doctor-patient relationship. Further, the industry has proclaimed, the laws and regulations are not necessary because the industry recognizes its social responsibilities and would live up to them, laws or no laws. The information presented here is at least a partial reply to such an argument. It demonstrates how some companies comport themselves when there are no restrictive laws, or when the laws are not enforced.

Solving the problem will be neither simple nor painless. No action by the Food and Drug Administration or the Congress of the United States, or by governmental bodies in Switzerland, France, Germany, and other drug-manufacturing countries, can yield an instant answer. In Latin America, more rigorous laws can be enacted, but these will be meaningless unless they are rigorously enforced. The global corporations, with or without pressure from their stockholders, should be induced to face up to their true social responsibilities. Physicians and scientists themselves should take a hand.

Regardless of the eventual solution, the first step must be the demonstration that the problem exists.

This investigation would have been totally impossible without the help, guidance, and dedication of many scores of friends and colleagues in the United States and throughout Latin America—private physicians and pharmacists, medical educators, researchers, government officials, ministers of health, and physicians and scientists within many of the drug companies themselves. Since the study began two years ago, they have given lavishly of their time, their knowledge, their ideas, their trust, and their hospitality. This book is a small expression of my gratitude.

Special thanks go to the following:

—in Mexico: DRS. SILVESTRE FRENK, EMILIO ROSENSTEIN, *and* LUIS SANCHEZ MEDAL.

—in Guatemala: DRS. RUBEN MAYORGA, CARLOS OVALLE, *and* JORGE ZUNIGA.

—in Costa Rica: DRS. FERNANDO MONTERO GEI, VIRGINIA RAMIREZ DE BARQUERO, *and* ALFONSO TREJOS WILLIS.

—in Colombia: DRS. GUSTAVO HITZIG BERGGRUN, HAROLDO CALVO NUNEZ, *and* JOSE FELIX PATINO.

—in Ecuador: DRS. RAUL MALDONADO MEJIA *and* JORGE REYES SALAS.

—in Brazil: TIMOTHY CROCKER.

—in Argentina: DR. JUAN E. NAVARRO CLARK.

And in the United States:

—DRS. JERE GOYAN, STEPHEN COHEN, LOUIS DIAMOND, EPHRAIM ENGLE-MAN, LEON EPSTEIN, ROBERT FISHMAN, ALAN MARGOLIS, *and* ROBERT N. SMITH *of the University of California, San Francisco.*

—DRS. PHILIP R. LEE, WALLACE EPSTEIN, MICHAEL GARLAND, JAN HOWARD, *and* ALBERT JONSEN, *and attorneys* LEWIS BUTLER *and* MICHAEL PARKER *of UCSF's Health Policy Program.*

—DRS. MARK NOVITCH *of the Food and Drug Administration and* LEON JACOBS *of the National Institutes of Health.*

—DR. LEO HOLLISTER *of the Veterans Administration Hospital at Palo Alto, California.*

—DR. JACK REMINGTON *of the Palo Alto Medical Research Foundation.*

—DR. WILLIAM L. HEWITT, JR., *of the University of California, Los Angeles.*

—PROFESSOR *and* MRS. ALVIN ZANDER *of the University of Michigan.*

—PETER BELL *of the Ford Foundation in New York and* JAMES HIMES, ALICIA GROOT, *and* RODOLFO LOW *in Ford's Bogotá office.*

—EDGAR ELFSTROM *of the "Daily News Tribune" in Fullerton, California,* RODNEY BEATON *of United Press International, and other newspapermen who gave priceless assistance.*

—*Attorney* CARLOS YNOSTROZA *of San Francisco, who provided great help in interpreting the laws of the Spanish-speaking countries, and attorney* MIGUEL LEITE, *also of San Francisco, who helped with the laws of Brazil.*

—*Officials of the following companies, who kindly reviewed for accuracy our translations of their Latin American promotional material: Johnson & Johnson, Eli Lilly, Lakeside, Lederle, McKesson, Merck Sharp & Dohme, Ortho, Parke-Davis, Sandoz, Schering, Searle, Smith Kline & French, Specia, Squibb, Syntex, Upjohn, Warner-Chilcott, and Winthrop.*

The inclusion of their names does not necessarily indicate that any of the above individuals approve or disapprove of the statements in this book.

Dr. Aida LeRoy, who served as a research assistant on this project, deserves full credit for translating the drug information from Spanish into English.

My particular thanks go to the Ford Foundation and the Janss Foundation, which provided financial support, much help, and absolutely no interference.

And finally, to Mia Lydecker for her unfailing assistance — *muchas gracias.*

MILTON SILVERMAN

San Francisco, October 12, 1975

A NOTE ABOUT THE AUTHOR

Milton Silverman, Ph.D., born in San Francisco in 1910, was trained in biochemistry and pharmacology at Stanford University and the University of California School of Medicine.

From 1934 to 1959, he won national recognition as science editor of the San Francisco *Chronicle,* and later as a science writer for the *Saturday Evening Post, Collier's, Reader's Digest,* and other magazines. He is a past-president of the National Association of Science Writers and a winner of the Lasker Award for distinguished medical reporting.

His own research has included studies on synthetic sugars, anesthetics, the pharmacology of alcoholic beverages, and cultural drinking patterns in South America, Europe, and the United States. For nearly a decade, he has been deeply involved in research on the discovery, production, promotion, pricing, prescribing, and use and misuse of prescription drugs. He has acted as a consultant to the U.S. Public Health Service and, on drug insurance policies, to the Social Security Administration and the House Ways and Means Committee.

From 1966 to 1969, he served as a special assistant to Philip R. Lee, M.D., Assistant Secretary for Health, in the Department of Health, Education, and Welfare, and as executive secretary of the HEW Task Force on Prescription Drugs. Since 1972, he has been a lecturer in pharmacology at the University of California's Schools of Pharmacy and Medicine in San Francisco, and a senior faculty member in UCSF's Health Policy Program.

He is the author of *Magic in a Bottle,* a history of drug research, and, with Dr. Lee as co-author, of *Pills, Profits, and Politics.*

1.

INTRODUCTION

It seems safe to assume that most physicians in whatever country they work do not prescribe drugs with any intention of needlessly harming a patient. If a drug is irrationally prescribed—the wrong drug for the wrong patient, in the wrong amounts, or at the wrong time, or if a drug is prescribed when no drug is needed—then the physician is presumably uninformed or misinformed. The necessary information may not be easily available; it may be available but ignored or misunderstood; it may be inaccurate, incomplete, or biased; or the physician may be swayed by patient pressure, peer pressure, or the intensive promotional campaign of the drug industry.[1]

In the United States, it may also be assumed that, for any prescription drug legally on the market, the essential information is available, complete, accurate, and—except for a few instances in which controversies remain unsettled—unbiased.

Since the enactment of the Kefauver-Harris Amendments in 1962 and their forceful implementation beginning in the mid-1960s, the U.S. Food and Drug Administration has taken significant steps to control the labeling, advertising, and other promotion of prescription drugs. It is now required that indications or claims of efficacy be limited to those that can be supported by what FDA considers to be substantial scientific evidence. Claims based essentially on endorsements, wide popularity among physicians, and many years of use—the so-called "test of time" argument—are no longer acceptable. Contraindications and warnings must be given in detail,† presented alongside

---

†Included in the descriptions of contraindications and warnings are statements which may be classified as "precautions" in certain of the reference volumes.

the approved indications. Potential adverse reactions, ranging from mild to lethal, must be fully disclosed. In addition, if previously unsuspected hazards are discovered, the drug manufacturer is required to notify all physicians promptly.

It is the official policy of FDA, and was presumably the intent of the Congress that enacted the legislation, that such regulations shall not control an individual physician in making his prescribing judgments. Instead, the regulations would enable him to make those judgments with maximum knowledge of the safety and efficacy of each product.

It has long been apparent that the policies followed in the United States have not been adopted universally. For example, in the congressional hearings on the drug industry conducted by Senator Gaylord Nelson, it was noted that the control of chloramphenicol advertising in British medical journals was far less stringent than that used in the United States.[2] As will be noted in the next chapter, notable differences in the labeling of chloramphenicol have also been found in many other countries.

To make a more extended comparison of prescription drug labeling and promotion, we have surveyed the published information presented to physicians and pharmacists on a number of important, widely used products marketed in various countries. For this report, we have selected twenty-eight drugs marketed in Latin America under a variety of brand or generic names by more than twenty multinational pharmaceutical companies. Many of these companies are based in the United States; others are based in Europe.

The products chosen for the study are presented in the next seven chapters on seven major categories: antibiotics, oral contraceptives, nonsteroid antiarthritics, steroid hormones, antipsychotic tranquilizers, antidepressants, and anticonvulsants.

In general, each product included here meets the following criteria: (a) it is a valuable and, in most instances, a widely used drug; (b) it is marketed in the United States and Latin America by the identical company or its foreign subsidiaries or affiliates; (c) it has well-established clinical usefulness and known hazards; and (d) it is described in the reference sources discussed below for the United States and for at least one of the Latin American countries. (No drug company is required to include its products in any of these volumes.) The descriptions of drugs marketed by domestic or nonglobal companies are, in general, the same as those given by the global firms, but they are not included here since they obviously provide no basis for international comparison.

The descriptive material presented in the following chapters is taken from the latest available editions of reference books distributed at no cost or sold to physicians. These include *Physicians' Desk Reference,* or *PDR,*[3] in the United States; *Diccionario de Especialidades Farmacéuticas, Edición Mexicana,*[4] in Mexico; *Diccionario de Especialidades Farmacéuticas, Edición C.A.D.,*[5] in the Central American countries — Guatemala, El Salvador, Honduras, Nicaragua, Costa Rica, and Panama — as well as the Dominican Republic; *Diccionario de Especialidades Farmacéuticas, Edición E. Co.,*[6] in Colombia and Ecuador; *Index Terapêutico Moderno,*[7] in Brazil; and *Therapia Vademecum,*[8] in Argentina. (The volumes for Mexico, Central America, and Colombia and Ecuador are commonly known to physicians as the PLMs, for *Para Los Medicos.*)

Other drug reference books are available to Latin American physicians, but these are generally far less comprehensive and do not include many products marketed by multinational companies.

PDR is used here as a standard of reference, not because the statements it contains — which reflect the attitudes of FDA and its expert consultants — are necessarily scientifically valid, endorsed by each drug manufacturer, or accepted by all physicians, or even by all expert physicians. Instead, *PDR* was selected as a basis for comparison because its drug descriptions are based on material that has been formally approved by an official government agency, they are at least tolerable to the drug manufacturers, and the volume is widely distributed to all practicing physicians in the United States and frequently consulted by them.[9] Under existing laws, the statements approved by FDA for each drug must form the basis for all package inserts, medical journal advertising, and other forms of labeling and promotion. The *PDR* listings themselves are considered to be both labeling and promotion, or a form of paid advertising distributed freely to physicians.[10]

As is the case with *PDR* in the United States, the *PLM* volumes for Mexico, Central America, and Colombia and Ecuador are distributed at no cost to physicians and are available for purchase by pharmacists and other health professionals.

There is apparently no question among physicians and government health officials—certainly in the United States[11]—that the drug descriptions these books contain are to be considered as anything but drug promotion or advertising, paid for by the drug companies that elect to list their products. In no country is any company, domestic or foreign, legally obliged to include its products.

"Generally," says Dr. Emilio Rosenstein, editor of the *PLM* books, "we invite the pharmaceutical companies to participate in the different editions by providing us with the description of the products they elect to list. The texts are almost always reviewed carefully by the medical directors of the firms." In Mexico it is theoretically necessary to have the prior approval of the Secretary of Health and Assistance for each description the laboratories wish distributed to physicians. In recent years, the government agency has urged that the product descriptions include mention of adverse reactions and contraindications. "At first," says Dr. Rosenstein, "this regulation encountered a certain amount of resistance, but most companies are beginning to accept the requirement, although they do not always extend themselves along these lines."†

For many years, Mexican laws have required that certain drugs may be dispensed only on a physician's prescription, while others—such as narcotics, antibiotics, antidiabetic agents, and potent analgesics—must carry at least some warning in the description. In the Mexican *PLM* volume, these matters are handled by a series of footnote references to a tabulation in the front of the book. One of these indicates "sale requires medical prescription," while another says simply "this medication is to be used with caution."

In Colombia, at least until recently, government control of information supplied by the companies to physicians has been minimal.‡ A similar situation has long existed in Ecuador. Practically no control over medical advertising and promotion has been exercised by the Central American countries.

The volume for Brazil indicates that the information on each product was furnished by the manufacturer, always based on texts

†A new health code, enacted in 1975, requires that adverse reactions and contraindications must be clearly mentioned in all publications, pamphlets, announcements, etc., destined for distribution to physicians. The type used for such warnings must be the same size as that used for describing indications.
‡This situation may be affected by new regulations which went into effect early in 1975. See Chapter 9.

approved by the government's Servicio de Fiscalizacão de Medicina e Farmácia. Each manufacturer was requested to provide physicians with all important information, including "composition, action, uses, dosages, administration, contraindications, precautions, danger, [and] side effects . . ." Physicians are advised that additional information may be obtained free of charge from the manufacturer.

"To our knowledge, Brazilian law does not require that promotional material be subjected to government approval," says Timothy Palmer, general manager of the firm that publishes the *Index.* "The medical directors of the individual laboratories, however, review the material painstakingly. Our editorial policy regarding disclosure of side-effects, etc., is very lenient, leaving these decisions to the participating company."

The situation in Argentina is quite different. As is not the case in the other countries concerned here, copies of *Therapia Vademecum* are available to physicians only by purchase. The Argentine volume contains an introductory statement noting that the material was prepared "without any advertising or financial support from the laboratories producing the medicinal specialties." The editors state that they present "an objective and impartial description of the preparations, being faithful to our policy of offering a complete information service without pretending to influence the prescription or administration of said products." The products selected for inclusion are chosen by the editors on the basis of their own criteria. The drug descriptions cannot be considered as drug advertising or propaganda.

"The texts are written by our staff as based on the available literature, both national and foreign," says Dr. Juan E. Navarro Clark, medical director of the publication. "We do not submit the material to the laboratories for their approval, although we may ask them to check for accuracy . . . The material produced by us is not supervised by any governmental agency."

For the background sections in each of the following chapters, there are many excellent authorities that could be cited as source material. For simplicity, we have elected to cite primarily two widely used and highly respected publications, Goodman and Gilman's *The Pharmacological Basis of Therapeutics*[12] and the American Medical Association's *AMA Drug Evaluations.*[13] It may be noted, however, that these two sources do not necessarily agree with *PDR* or, for that matter, with each other.

In this introductory section, there are four points that deserve special emphasis:

— The problem of drug misuse is now receiving worldwide attention. This problem is presumably aggravated by the fact that many potent products obtainable in the United States and most European countries only with a physician's prescription can be purchased over-the-counter without a prescription in the Latin American countries.

— The practices described in this report — the exaggerating of claims and the glossing-over of hazards — are not limited to Latin America. They do not represent an approach used only in the industrially underdeveloped nations. As we will mention later, similar practices — involving equally serious clinical and ethical problems — may be observed in economically advanced countries.

— Nothing in this book is intended to approve or condemn the drug labeling and promotional regulations set by FDA.

— Finally, and of particular importance, the comments included here are intended in no way to pass judgment on the relative training, skill, competence, or dedication of physicians or pharmacists in the United States and Latin America, or on their ability to make rational judgments based on readily available information. What is considered here is the adequacy and reliability of the information presented to them.

2.

ANTIBIOTICS

Four antibiotics were selected for study. These are:

— chloramphenicol (marketed by Parke-Davis as Chloromycetin, by Winthrop as Wintetil, by McKesson as Cloranfenicol MK and Cloramfenicol MK, and by Boehringer as Cloranfenicol "Cloranficina")

— tetracycline (marketed by Lederle as Achromycin and Acromicina)

— amphotericin B (marketed by Squibb as Fungizone, Fungizon, and Amfostat)

— gentamicin (marketed by Schering as Garamycin and Garamicina, and by Essex as Gentamina)

CLINICAL BACKGROUND

It should be beyond question that antibiotics are among the most valuable pharmaceutical products available to modern physicians. On the other hand, it is now becoming evident that they are among the most misprescribed drugs, and increasing concern is being expressed by medical groups, FDA, and other agencies examining either or both the clinical aspects and the economic costs of prescription drugs.

Too often, it has been held, antibiotics and other antimicrobials are prescribed when they are clinically unnecessary or worthless, as in the treatment of the common cold or the "flu," or in many cases "to prevent complications." In some instances, especially in elective surgery, antibiotics may be given as a routine prophylaxis to every patient in what has been described as a "pharmaceutical version of

propitiating the gods."[1] Some potentially toxic antibiotics are prescribed when equally effective but safer substances are available. Some
antibiotics are used against strains of micro-organisms that are
resistant to them. Some highly expensive products are used when
equally safe and effective but less costly drugs are available.

The extent of these practices has been the subject of many studies in
recent years. For example, Roberts and Visconti reported one survey
conducted on 1,035 hospitalized patients of whom 340 had been given
antimicrobial therapy. A review team judged that the treatment had
been rational in 12.9 percent of the cases, questionable in 21.5
percent, and irrational—wrong drug, wrong dosage, wrong route of
administration, or no drug indicated in the first place—in 65.6
percent.[2] In another study, Maronde reported that cephalexin had
been prescribed irrationally for fifty of fifty-four patients.[3] Stolley and
Lasagna have reported that about 95 percent of physicians will issue
one or more prescriptions to a patient diagnosed as suffering from a
common cold. Almost 60 percent of these prescriptions are for
antibiotics.[4]

If these antibiotics were useless but harmless, their irrational
prescription might be clinically acceptable if only for their placebo
effect, though economically unjustified. No antibiotic, however, may
be judged innocuous. Each has a potentially toxic effect, serious or
life-threatening, on the individual. In addition, widespread and
intensive application of antibiotics—especially in hospitals—has been
blamed as at least a contributing factor in the appearance of resistant
strains of organisms causing many thousands of deaths a year in the
United States from gram-negative bacteremias alone.[5]

In addition, for the four drugs discussed here, there are particular
hazards that deserve consideration.

Chloramphenicol

Since 1951, the potential hazards of chloramphenicol—especially in
causing serious or fatal blood dyscrasias—have been stressed repeated-
ly in warnings by such groups as the American Medical Association,[6-8]
the National Academy of Sciences/National Research Council[9] and
FDA,[10] and by various individual medical authorities.[11-14] As a result,
the indiscriminate use of this antibiotic is strongly discouraged in the

United States. In the American Medical Association's *AMA Drug Evaluations*, it is stated: "Although chloramphenicol is an effective agent, its potential hematotoxicity makes other antibacterial agents preferred in certain infections."[15]

Companies marketing chloramphenicol in the United States are now required to warn against its use in "trivial infections." Some observers have suggested that such a warning is far too gentle, since a physician may well assume that any patient seeking his professional care is obviously afflicted with a nontrivial illness. Instead, these observers have said, the warnings for chloramphenicol should restrict its use to "life-threatening" infections in which the causative organism is known to be sensitive to this drug.

Chloramphenicol figured in an unprecedented episode when, in August 1968, the Pan American Health Organization (an arm of the World Health Organization) transmitted to all Latin American countries a warning against its unjustified use.[16] These warnings had already been transmitted by FDA and the *Journal of the American Medical Association* to all physicians in the United States. In June 1971, the Director-General of WHO sent all member nations a copy of the FDA regulations on such warnings.[17] In May 1972, PAHO dispatched a special memorandum on the subject to all Latin American countries.[18] The WHO and PAHO moves had little if any significant impact in Latin America.

The Latin American countries are by no means the only ones in which at least some drug companies have minimized the hazards of chloramphenicol. The same thing occurs in some highly developed nations. In a recent survey covering the United States and twenty other countries (none in Latin America), Dunne et al. reported striking differences in the labeling of Chloromycetin by Parke-Davis.[19] The promotion of chloramphenicol products by various companies in Japan has recently been criticized by Hellegers.[20]

Tetracycline

It is generally accepted that the tetracyclines as a group are of relatively low toxicity when used in the recommended doses, but some potentially serious side effects must be considered. Superinfections have occurred, and these may be life-threatening. Liver damage may occur when certain tetracyclines are given even for short periods to normal patients, those who are pregnant, or those with renal or hepatic insufficiency, or when other potentially hepatotoxic agents are given at the same time. Administration to children less than seven to ten years of age may result in interference with normal tooth and bone development.[21],[22]

Amphotericin B

Squibb's amphotericin B is the only drug available for treatment of some particularly serious systemic fungal infections. It is, however, relatively toxic, and a large number and variety of untoward effects have been associated with its use. More than 80 percent of patients treated with this agent develop decreased renal function.[23] In most cases, the decrease is reversible after termination of treatment.

Gentamicin

A relatively new antibiotic, gentamicin is believed to have its most important applications in the treatment of gram-negative bacterial infections. It is especially effective in infections caused by *Pseudomonas aeruginosa, Enterobacter, Klebsiella,* and other species resistant to more widely used agents.[24] It may damage the kidney and the auditory and vestibular portions of the eighth cranial nerve.[25] Ototoxicity appears in about 2 percent of patients, with vestibular function more susceptible to damage than hearing. The risk is highest in patients with renal insufficiency.[26]

LABELING

Chloramphenicol

The background material presented above on chloramphenicol is clearly reflected in the statements published in *PDR* for the information of physicians and pharmacists in the United States (Table 1). Large type is used to indicate that this antibiotic should be restricted to use in serious or life-threatening infections when less potentially dangerous drugs are ineffective or contraindicated. It should not be prescribed for the treatment of trivial infections or where it is not indicated, as in the case of the common cold, the "flu," and infections of the throat, or as a prophylactic agent to prevent infections. Emphasis is placed on the fact that its demonstrated hazards include the possibility of producing a highly fatal aplastic anemia or other blood dyscrasia.

Latin American physicians, however, are told that the indications for Parke-Davis' Chloromycetin, Winthrop's Wintetil,† McKesson's Cloranfenicol MK and Cloramfenicol MK, and Boehringer's Cloranfenicol "Cloranficina" include not only such diseases as typhoid fever, but also tonsillitis, pharyngitis, whooping cough, abscesses, gonorrhea, pneumonia, and ulcerative colitis. In some of the Latin American descriptions, few or no warnings or adverse reactions are disclosed.

The companies whose products are considered above are by no means the only ones describing chloramphenicol as indicated for a wide range of conditions. In one publication distributed to physicians in Bolivia, Chile, Ecuador, Paraguay, Peru, Uruguay, and Venezuela, the Ecuador-based firm Acromax lists the following indications for its product Acromaxfenicol: typhoid fever, paratyphoid and other salmonelloses, staphylococcic infections, bacillary dysentery, urinary infections due to bacilli and cocci, undulant fever, pneumonia and other respiratory and bacillary infections, rickettsiosis, murine typhus, blennorrhagia, such spirochete infections as yaws and syphilis, lymphogranuloma venereum, psittacosis, trachoma, whooping cough, meningitis, eye and ear infections, skin infections, and surgical infections. For contraindications and warnings, it mentions only "hematopathies" and recommends that frequent blood tests be carried out in prolonged treatments. No adverse reactions are listed.[27]

Tetracycline

As shown in Table 2, physicians in the United States are informed of the organisms causing infections for which the use of tetracycline has been supported by substantial scientific evidence. Their colleagues in Mexico and Argentina are given a list of disease conditions in which it is indicated. Physicians in Central America and Brazil, however, are told only that Lederle's product is a "broad spectrum antibiotic."

In the Lederle product description in *PDR*, considerable space is

†This product was removed from the market in 1972.

devoted to a discussion of contraindications, warnings, and potential adverse reactions, including the possibility of interference with bone and tooth development in children, liver damage, and overgrowth of nonsusceptible organisms. In the comparable reference volumes in Mexico, Central America, Brazil, and Argentina, such matters are mentioned only briefly or not at all.

Amphotericin B

For the relatively toxic amphotericin B — Squibb's Fungizone, Fungizon, or Amfostat — United States physicians are advised to use the drug primarily for progressive, life-threatening fungus infections, but never simply on a diagnosis based on a skin or serologic test without clinical evidence of disease (Table 3). This warning is implied but not emphasized in Latin American countries, though it would seem most needed there, where large segments of the population normally react positively to such a test, usually because of an earlier fungus infection.[28] Serious or potentially fatal side effects of amphotericin B are spelled out in detail in the United States but minimized or not mentioned in the other countries.

Gentamicin

Serious adverse reactions caused by gentamicin products — Schering's Garamycin or Garamicina and Essex's Gentamina — are described in detail in the United States but minimized in Latin America (Table 4).

TABLE 1. *Information given on:*

CHLORAMPHENICOL
marketed as CHLOROMYCETIN (Parke-Davis), WINTETIL (Winthrop),* CLOR-ANFENICOL MK, CLORAMFENICOL MK (McKesson), CLORANFENICOL "CLORANFICINA" (Boehringer).

	Parke-Davis				Winthrop	McKesson		Boehringer
	U.S.A.	Mexico	Central America	Argentina	Central America	Central America	Ecuador, Colombia	Brazil
INDICATIONS FOR USE:								
Acute typhoid fever	✓	✓	✓	✓		✓		✓
Salmonella infections	✓a	✓	✓	✓		✓		✓
Hemophilus influenzae infections	✓a	✓	✓	✓		✓		
Rickettsial infections	✓a	✓	✓	✓		✓		
Lymphogranuloma-psittacosis group	✓a	✓	✓					
Gram-negative bacteremia, meningitis	✓a							
Organisms resistant to other agents	✓a							
Cystic fibrosis regimens	✓							
Enteric, dysenteric infections *(Shigella)*		✓	✓	✓		✓		
Laryngotracheobronchitis, tonsillitis, pharyngitis		✓	✓					
Urinary tract, uterine, surgical, ophthalmic infections, peritonitis		✓	✓					
Tularemia, bacterial pneumonias		✓	✓					
Brucellosis		✓	✓	✓				
Ulcerative colitis, abscesses, phlebitis		✓	✓					
Relapsing fever, yaws, spirochetes		✓	✓	✓				
Suppurative otitis media		✓	✓					
Whooping cough						✓		
Staphylococcal, streptococcal, pneumococcal, gonococcal,								

TABLE 1 Continued.

	Parke-Davis				Win-throp	McKesson		Boehr-inger
	U.S.A.	Mexico	Central America	Argentina	Central America	Central America	Ecuador, Colombia	Brazil
INDICATIONS FOR USE, Continued								
Pseudomonas aeruginosa, _Actinomyces_ infections				✓				
"Generally infections due to susceptible organisms"						✓		✓
"Broad spectrum antibiotic"					✓			
"Anti-infective agent"							✓	
CONTRAINDICATIONS AND WARNINGS:								
Contraindicated if previous hypersensitivity or toxic reactions	✓	✓						
Contraindicated if depression of bone marrow	✓	✓						
Avoid concurrent use with other drugs that may depress bone marrow	✓							
Perform baseline blood studies, repeat at approximately 2-day intervals	✓							
Serial blood studies if administration more than one week		✓						
Periodic blood studies in prolonged treatment					✓			✓
"Perform frequent blood studies"						✓		
Discontinue if signs of blood dyscrasia	✓					✓		✓
Avoid repeated courses of treatment	✓							
Discontinue treatment soon as possible	✓							
Caution in impaired liver, kidney function	✓							
Caution in pregnancy, lactation	✓							

TABLE 1 Continued.

	Parke-Davis				Win-throp	McKesson		Boehr-inger
	U.S.A.	Mexico	Central America	Argentina	Central America	Central America	Ecuador, Colombia	Brazil
CONTRAINDICATIONS AND WARNINGS, Continued								
Caution in premature or full-term infants	✓							
Overgrowth of nonsusceptible organisms	✓							
NONE LISTED			X	X			X	
ADVERSE REACTIONS:								
Aplastic anemia, other blood dyscrasias[b]	✓	✓				✓		✓
Nausea, vomiting, other GI reactions	✓							
Headache, mild depression, mental confusion, other neurologic reactions	✓							
Hypersensitivity reactions	✓							
Gray syndrome in premature and newborn infants[b]	✓							
NONE LISTED			X	X	X		X	

*Removed from market in 1972.

[a]Only in serious infections caused by susceptible strains.

[b]Potentially fatal.

NOTE: Explanation of the sources of information in this table will be found on page ix.

TABLE 2. *Information given on:*

TETRACYCLINE

marketed as ACHROMYCIN, ACROMICINA (Lederle).

	U.S.A.	Mexico	Central America	Brazil	Argentina
INDICATIONS FOR USE:					
Rickettsiae infections	√				√
Mycoplasma pneumoniae infections	√				
Psittacosis, ornithosis infections	√				
Lymphogranuloma venereum, granuloma inguinale	√				
Borrelia recurrentis (relapsing fever)	√				
Hemophilus ducreyi (chancroid)	√				√
Vibrio comma, Vibrio fetus, Bartonella bacilliformis	√				
Brucella species	√	√			
Bacteroides species, *Escherichia coli*	√				
Enterobacter aerogenes; Mima, Herellea species	√				
Shigella species	√	√			
Hemophilus influenzae (respiratory infections)	√				
Klebsiella species (respiratory and urinary infections)	√				
Streptococcus pyogenes	√[a]				
Streptococcus (alpha-hemolytic)	√				
Enterococcus group, *Diplococcus pneumoniae*	√				
Staphylococcus aureus	√[b]				
Neisseria gonorrhea	√[b]	√			
Treponema pallidum	√[b]				√
Treponema pertenue	√[b]				
Listeria monocytogenes, Clostridium species	√[b]				
Bacillus anthracis, Fusobacterium fusiforme	√[b]				
Actinomyces species	√[b]				
Conjunctivitis	√	√			
Trachoma	√				
Acne	√[c]	√			
Acute intestinal amebiasis	√[c]				
Pasteurella pestis, Pasteurella tularensis	√				
Pneumonitis, bronchitis, tonsillitis, otitis, biliary infections		√			
Infectious diarrheas, pyelonephritis, cystitis		√			

TABLE 2 Continued.

	U.S.A.	Mexico	Central America	Brazil	Argentina
INDICATIONS FOR USE, Continued					
Bacterial endocarditis		✓			✓
Phlebitis, abscesses, wound infections, cellulitis		✓			
Typhoid, rheumatic fever		✓			
Styes, measles		✓			
Gram-negative, Gram-positive sepsis					✓
Protozoa, certain viruses					✓
Respiratory, genitourinary, soft tissue infections					✓
Typhous syndrome, meningitis, septicemia					✓
Operative prophylaxis					✓
"Broad spectrum antibiotic"		✓			✓
"All infections sensitive to broad spectrum antibiotic"				✓	
CONTRAINDICATIONS AND WARNINGS:					
Hypersensitivity to any tetracycline	✓				
Caution in pregnancy, infancy, children	✓	✓		✓	
Caution in renal impairment[d]	✓				
Caution in liver impairment	✓				
Photosensitivity	✓	✓			
Caution in premature infants, lactating mothers	✓				
Overgrowth of nonsusceptible organisms	✓	✓		✓	
Interference with anticoagulant therapy	✓				
Avoid using with penicillin	✓				
Other potentially hepatotoxic drugs should not be prescribed concomitantly	✓				
Do periodic studies of hematopoietic, renal, hepatic systems in long-term therapy	✓				
Dental staining in infants, children	✓	✓		✓	
Contraindicated in hemorrhagic states, albuminuria, hematuria, anaphylactic shock		✓			
Contraindicated in gastritis, vaginitis, glossitis, dermatitis, stomatitis		✓			
"Idiosyncrasy"					✓
NONE LISTED			X		

TABLE 2 Continued.

	U.S.A.	Mexico	Central America	Brazil	Argentina
ADVERSE REACTIONS:					
Vomiting, diarrhea, nausea, other gastrointestinal disturbances	✓	✓		✓	
Rashes, other skin reactions	✓			✓	
Renal toxicity	✓				
Hypersensitivity reactions	✓				
Toxic effects on fetus	✓				
Blood changes	✓				
Vaginitis				✓	
NONE LISTED			X		X

aNot drug of choice in upper respiratory infections.

bNot drug of choice.

cAdjunct in severe forms.

dPotentially fatal.

NOTE: Explanation of the sources of information in this table will be found on page ix.

TABLE 3. *Information given on:*

AMPHOTERICIN B

marketed as FUNGIZONE, FUNGIZON, AMFOSTAT (Squibb).

	U.S.A.	Mexico	Central America	Brazil	Argentina
INDICATIONS FOR USE:					
Cryptococcosis (torulosis)	√a	√		√	√
Blastomycosis	√a	√		√	√
Disseminated forms of moniliasis	√a	√		√	√
Coccidoidomycosis, histoplasmosis	√a	√		√	√
Mucormycosis (phycomycosis)	√a				
Sporotrichosis, aspergillosis	√a				
American leishmaniasis	√a,b			√	√
Disseminated mycotic infections			√		
CONTRAINDICATIONS AND WARNINGS:					
Not for use in inapparent fungal disease which shows only positive skin or serological test	√				
Hypersensitivity to drug	√	√	√	√	
Parenteral use only in hospitalized patient or under close clinical observation	√	√			
Reduce dosage if toxic reactions	√			√	√
Caution in concurrent use of corticosteroids, nephrotoxic antibiotics, antineoplastic agents	√				
Weekly blood studies, etc., advisable	√				
In prolonged therapy, periodic test of hepatic, renal, bone marrow function advisable					√
Caution in pregnancy	√				
ADVERSE REACTIONS:					
Fever (sometimes with shaking chills), headache, nausea, vomiting	√	√		√	√
Anorexia, malaise, muscle and joint pain, cramping epigastric pain, diarrhea, hypokalemia	√	√		√	
Weight loss, dyspepsia	√				
Venous pain at injection site, with phlebitis and thrombophlebitis	√	√		√	

TABLE 3 Continued.

	U.S.A.	Mexico	Central America	Brazil	Argentina
ADVERSE REACTIONS, Continued					
Temporary or permanent abnormal renal function	✓			✓	
Anaphylactoid reactions	✓			✓	
Acute liver failure	✓				
Anuria, coagulation defects, miscellaneous blood dyscrasias	✓				
Cardiovascular toxicity (cardiac arrest, etc.)	✓				✓
Rashes, miscellaneous neurological symptoms	✓	✓		✓	
NONE LISTED			X		

aPrimarily for progressive, potentially fatal form.
bNot drug of choice.
NOTE: Explanation of the sources of information in this table will be found on page ix.

TABLE 4. *Information given on:*

GENTAMICIN

marketed as GARAMYCIN, GARAMICINA (Schering), GENTAMINA (Essex).

	U.S.A.	Mexico	Central America	Ecuador, Colombia	Brazil	Argentina
INDICATIONS FOR USE:						
In serious infections caused by susceptible strains	√	√	√	√	√	√
Pseudomonas aeruginosa; Escherichia coli	√	√	√	√	√	√
Proteus species	√	√	√	√	√	√
Klebsiella, Enterobacter, Serratia species	√	√	√	√	√	√
Staphylococcus	√	√	√	√	√	√
Shigella, Salmonella		√	√	√	√	√
Streptococcus (group A beta-hemolytic)	√[a]				√	√
Neisseria gonorrhoeae		√		√		
Septicemia, Gram-negative and Gram-positive	√	√	√	√	√	√
Central nervous system infections (meningitis)	√	√	√	√	√	√
Urinary tract, respiratory tract infections	√	√	√	√	√	√
Gastrointestinal tract infections	√	√	√	√	√	√
Skin and soft tissue infections, peritonitis	√	√	√	√	√	√
Burn and graft infections	√	√	√	√	√	√
Neonatal staphylococcal pneumonia	√[a]					
Postsurgical infections, wound infections, septic abortions		√				
Osseous tissue infections		√				
Neonatal bacteremia	√	√	√	√	√	√
Drug of choice in infections when causative agent not yet identified			√	√		√
CONTRAINDICATIONS AND WARNINGS:						
Hypersensitivity to drug	√	√	√[b]		√[b]	
Ototoxicity	√	√	√[b]	√[c]	√[b]	√
Caution in patients with renal impairment	√	√[c]	√	√[c]	√[c]	√
Caution in patients taking ototoxic or other neurotoxic drugs	√	√	√	√[c]	√	√
Caution in patients taking nephrotoxic drugs	√	√				

TABLE 4 Continued.

	U.S.A.	Mexico	Central America	Ecuador,Colombia	Brazil	Argentina
CONTRAINDICATIONS AND WARNINGS, Continued						
Caution in patients taking neuromuscular blocking agents	√	√				
Caution in patients taking potent diuretics	√	√				
Overgrowth of nonsusceptible organisms	√		√b		√b	
Caution in pregnancy	√	√		√c	√c	√
Caution in newborn	√			√c	√c	√
ADVERSE REACTIONS:						
Renal toxicity	√	√	√d			√
Ototoxicity—vestibular	√	√	√	√	√e	√
Ototoxicity—auditory	√	√			√	√
Numbness, skin tingling, muscle twitching, convulsions	√f					
Blood changes (anemia, granulocytopenia, etc.)	√f					
Fever, rash, itching, urticaria, joint pain	√					
Cutaneous hypersensitivity reactions		√	√		√b	
Nausea, vomiting, headache, lethargy	√f					
Decreased appetite, weight loss	√f					
Blood pressure changes	√f					

aWith penicillin-type drug as adjuvant.
bRarely occurs.
cUse only when infection is life-threatening.
dUsually reversible.
eInfrequent.
fPossibly related to drug.
NOTE: Explanation of the sources of information in this table will be found on page ix.

3.

ORAL CONTRACEPTIVES

Included here are a number of combination products widely prescribed for use as oral contraceptives:

—ethynodiol diacetate + mestranol (marketed by Searle as Ovulen)

—norethindrone acetate + ethinyl estradiol (marketed by Parke-Davis as Norlestrin and Prolestrin)

—norethindrone + mestranol (marketed by Ortho as Ortho Novum, by Johnson as Novulon, and by Syntex as Norinyl)

—norgestrel + ethinyl estradiol (marketed by Wyeth as Ovral and Anfertil)

CLINICAL BACKGROUND

In recent years, probably no other drugs have stirred up more controversy than have the oral contraceptives. The use and the promotion of these agents have been at the center of clinical, sociological, ethical, religious, and even political disputes which remain unsettled.[1] In at least some respects, the oral contraceptives are unique. They may be taken by millions of women throughout their entire childbearing period. They are used as medicinal substances by individuals who presumably are in good health. Their efficacy in the prevention of pregnancy appears to be well established, but their long-term safety—for example, over a period of twenty years or more—remains unknown.

From the outset, the safety of oral contraceptives has been a matter of heated argument. Proponents of The Pill have declared that using oral contraceptives is safer than driving on the highways, but the relevancy of this comparison is not clear. It has been claimed that The Pill is safer than pregnancy, but it would seem more reasonable that oral contraceptives should properly be compared for both safety and efficacy not with pregnancy but with other contraceptive methods. The first drug companies marketing oral contraceptives were strongly criticized for failing to disclose their hazards.[2] On the other hand, advocates of The Pill — and especially those concerned with the success of nationwide or even worldwide family planning programs — have asserted that widespread dissemination of information on the hazards of The Pill would only frighten many women from using it and thus intensify the world population crisis. A recent four-year survey, covering 23,000 users and 23,000 controls, has indicated that the hazards of The Pill are minimal, but they are real.[3]

One dispute has centered on how much information on the known hazards of oral contraceptives should be divulged to the patient. In 1970, the Food and Drug Administration decided that the patient was entitled to such knowledge. Accordingly, FDA ruled that each package of oral contraceptives should contain a suitable information statement directed toward the women who were considering their use. This move was denounced by the American Medical Association as an unwarranted interference in doctor-patient relationships, but nonetheless it was put into effect.[4]

How much information should be given to the patient may be one matter. How much should be given to the physician, the pharmacist, or other health professionals is quite different. Presumably it is mainly on the basis of this information furnished to the physician that he can appropriately advise each patient on which, if any, contraceptive method she should apply, how she should use it with maximum safety and efficacy, and what special precautions and follow-up procedures the physician himself should employ.

Some of the variations may reflect conflicting views within the medical and scientific communities. Thus, in the United States, FDA has held that there is substantial evidence to support the use of these products for the prevention of pregnancy. On the other hand, some investigators have claimed that oral contraceptives are also effective for control of acne, premenstrual tension, menstrual pain, and menopausal symptoms, but *AMA Drug Evaluations* has stated there is no justification at present for prescribing them for such purposes. Some investigators have also claimed that these contraceptives are effective in the control of such conditions as hypogonadism with primary amenorrhea, secondary amenorrhea, dysfunctional uterine bleeding, and endometriosis.[5] FDA has approved the use of high potency oral contraceptives for dysfunctional uterine bleeding and endometriosis.

LABELING

In the United States, the information contained in *PDR* on all combination oral contraceptives is virtually the same.

As indicated in Table 5, one clinical application is approved for this group of agents: contraception. In general, they are not recommended for the treatment of premenstrual tension, menstrual pain, menstrual irregularities, functional infertility, the discomforts of the menopause, or any other gynecological condition. With certain high potency products, however, use is approved in hypermenorrhea and endometriosis.

The list of contraindications and warnings is lengthy, detailed, and specific, with particular attention placed on past or present thrombophlebitis, thromboembolism, impaired liver function, known *or suspected* estrogen-dependent malignancies, and unexplained abnormal genital bleeding. Physicians are urged to be alert to the earliest signs of thrombotic disorders, changes in the eye or optic nerve, migraine, changes in cardiac or renal function, increase in blood pressure, changes in carbohydrate tolerance, and any increase in depression or other psychic manifestation. Physicians are likewise advised to conduct periodic examinations of the breasts and pelvic organs, including routine vaginal smear tests for cancer.

In the same manner, potential adverse reactions are presented in considerable detail, including such manifestations as change in libido, headache, nervousness, dizziness, fatigue, backache, hirsutism, loss of hair, rashes, and other skin changes. The possible interference of these contraceptive agents in a wide variety of diagnostic tests is described.

This relatively complete portrayal of information, required by law in the United States, is not found in other countries.

Ovulen

In Mexico, as in the United States, Searle's Ovulen is indicated solely for the prevention of pregnancy. In Central America, Colombia, and Brazil, it is described more or less explicitly as a contraceptive, and in Argentina to provide "ovulatory rest," but in some countries it is also indicated for such conditions as premenstrual tension, menstrual pain, menopausal discomfort, and other gynecological conditions.

In most of the Latin American countries, contraindications are generally limited to a *proven* history of liver disease, mammary or genital tract cancer, thrombophlebitis, or cerebral vascular disease. In Colombia, however, only cancer is given as a contraindication.

A few adverse reactions are noted in Mexico and Central America, but none is listed in Colombia, Brazil, or Argentina.

Norlestrin, Prolestrin

Marketed as Norlestrin in the United States, Central America, Colombia, Ecuador, and Argentina, and as Prolestrin in Mexico, this Parke-Davis product is described with essentially the same indications, including not only the voluntary control of ovulation, but also — in the Latin American countries — the treatment of premenstrual tension, menstrual pain, endocrine infertility, and other menstrual or gynecological disorders.

In Mexico, Colombia, and Ecuador, the product is described as contraindicated in patients with a thromboembolic background or in those with hormone-dependent malignancies. Liver disease is not given as a contraindication. No contraindications are mentioned in Central America or Argentina.

Potential adverse reactions are presented mainly as transient or unimportant phenomena in Mexico, Colombia, and Ecuador, but no such reactions are listed in Central America or Argentina.

Ortho Novum, Novulon

Ortho's Ortho Novum is listed in the United States and Mexico as a contraceptive and in Central America as a control for ovulation. The Johnson product is marketed in Brazil and Argentina as Novulon. In Brazil, it is described as useful to prevent ovulation, normalize the

menstrual cycle, and control dysmenorrhea, cyclical uterine hemorrhage, and endometriosis. In Argentina, it is listed as useful for the
"transitory and reversible inhibition of ovulation" and also for
treatment of a variety of menstrual disorders.

Contraindications and warnings are presented in some detail for
both products. In Argentina, it is recommended that any patient using
the drug should be examined by a physician every six months. For
Ortho Novum, the listed adverse reactions are indicated to be of
relatively minor importance and generally transitory in nature. For
Novulon, as marketed in Brazil, a limited list of potential adverse
reactions, most of these apparently of minor importance, is included.
In Argentina, no adverse reactions are listed.

Norinyl

This Syntex product, with the same active ingredients as Ortho Novum
and Novulon, is described in the United States and Mexico as
indicated only for the suppression of ovulation. The contraindications
and warnings and the possible adverse reactions are identical with
those listed in Mexico for Ortho Novum.

Ovral, Anfertil

Wyeth's Ovral, also marketed in Brazil as Anfertil, is recommended in
the Latin American countries not only for the control or inhibition of
ovulation but also for the treatment of a wide variety of menstrual
disorders. In the United States it is described only as for the prevention
of pregnancy.

In Colombia, Ecuador, and Brazil, Ovral is contraindicated for
patients with a confirmed history of liver disease, thrombophlebitis, or
hormone-dependent neoplasms. In Colombia and Ecuador, psychosis
and even suspected genital or mammary carcinoma are also considered to be contraindications. Brazilian physicians are told that there
are no known contraindications when Ovral is prescribed to "healthy
patients." In Argentina, contraindications include only the vague
statement that the drug has the same contraindications and warnings
that apply to other oral contraceptives.

No adverse reactions are listed in Colombia, Ecuador, Brazil, or
Argentina.

TABLE 5. *Information given on:*

ORAL CONTRACEPTIVES

marketed as OVULEN (Searle), NORLESTRIN, PROLESTRIN (Parke-Davis), ORTHO NOVUM (Ortho), NOVULON (Johnson), NORINYL (Syntex), OVRAL, ANFERTIL (Wyeth).

INDICATIONS FOR USE:	Ovulen						Norlestrin, Prolestrin					Ortho Novum, Novulon					Norinyl		Ovral, Anfertil			
	U.S.A.	Mexico	Central America	Ecuador/Colombia	Brazil	Argentina	U.S.A.	Mexico	Central America	Ecuador/Colombia	Argentina	U.S.A.	Mexico	Central America	Brazil	Argentina	U.S.A.	Mexico	U.S.A.	Ecuador/Colombia	Brazil	Argentina
Contraception	✓	✓	✓	✓	✓	✓	✓	✓	✓	✓	✓	✓	✓	✓	✓	✓	✓	✓	✓	✓	✓	✓
Regularization of menstrual cycle			✓					✓	✓	✓	✓											
Premenstrual tension			✓	✓				✓	✓	✓	✓				✓ⁿ	✓ⁿ					✓	✓
Dysmenorrhea			✓	✓				✓	✓	✓	✓				✓ⁿ	✓ⁿ						
Menopausal problems						✓		✓	✓	✓	✓											
Endocrine infertility											✓											
Endometriosis												✓ⁿ			✓ⁿ	✓ⁿ					✓	
Hypermenorrhea			✓		✓	✓		✓	✓	✓	✓	✓ⁿ				✓ⁿ					✓	
Miscellaneous menstrual disorders								✓	✓	✓	✓									✓	✓	✓
Uterine bleeding															✓ⁿ					✓	✓	✓

ⁿ = a

TABLE 5 Continued.

CONTRAINDICATIONS AND WARNINGS:	Ovulen						Norlestrin, Prolestrin					Ortho Novum, Novulon					Norinyl		Ovral, Anfertil			
	U.S.A.	Mexico	Central America	Ecuador, Colombia	Brazil	Argentina	U.S.A.	Mexico	Central America	Ecuador, Colombia	Argentina	U.S.A.	Mexico	Central America	Brazil	Argentina	U.S.A.	Mexico	U.S.A.	Ecuador, Colombia	Brazil	Argentina
Thromboembolic (thrombophlebitis, apoplexy, pulmonary embolism, retinal embolism)	✓	✓	✓		✓	✓	✓	✓		✓		✓	✓	✓	✓		✓	✓	✓	✓	✓	
Suspected hormone-dependent neoplasm	✓						✓					✓		✓		✓	✓		✓	✓		
Proved hormone-dependent neoplasm	✓	✓	✓	✓		✓	✓	✓		✓		✓	✓	✓	✓	✓	✓	✓	✓		✓	
Impaired liver function	✓	✓	✓			✓	✓					✓	✓	✓	✓	✓	✓	✓	✓	✓	✓	
Undiagnosed abnormal vaginal bleeding	✓						✓					✓	✓	✓	✓		✓	✓	✓			
Emotional disease	✓						✓					✓			✓		✓		✓	✓		

29

TABLE 5 Continued.

	Ovulen						Norlestrin, Prolestrin					Ortho Novum, Novulon					Norinyl		Ovral, Anfertil			
	U.S.A.	Mexico	Central America	Ecuador, Colombia	Brazil	Argentina	U.S.A.	Mexico	Central America	Ecuador, Colombia	Argentina	U.S.A.	Mexico	Central America	Brazil	Argentina	U.S.A.	Mexico	U.S.A.	Ecuador, Colombia	Brazil	Argentina
CONTRAINDICATIONS AND WARNINGS, Continued																						
Regular breast, pelvic examination	✓						✓					✓				✓	✓		✓			
Caution in epilepsy, migraine, asthma, cardiac or renal dysfunction	✓						✓					✓		✓	✓	✓	✓		✓			
NONE LISTED									✕		✕											✕
ADVERSE REACTIONS:																						
Thromboembolic	✓						✓	✓		✓		✓					✓		✓			
Nausea, gastrointestinal symptoms	✓	✓	✓				✓					✓			✓		✓		✓			
Breakthrough bleeding	✓	✓	✓				✓					✓	✓		✓		✓	✓	✓			
Menstrual irregularities	✓	✓	✓				✓					✓	✓	✓	✓		✓	✓	✓			

TABLE 5 Continued.

ADVERSE REACTIONS, Continued	Ovulen						Norlestrin, Prolestrin					Ortho Novum, Novulon					Norinyl		Ovral, Anfertil			
	U.S.A.	Mexico	Central America	Ecuador,Colombia	Brazil	Argentina	U.S.A.	Mexico	Central America	Ecuador,Colombia	Argentina	U.S.A.	Mexico	Central America	Brazil	Argentina	U.S.A.	Mexico	U.S.A.	Ecuador,Colombia	Brazil	Argentina
Breast changes	✓	✓	✓				✓					✓	✓		✓		✓	✓	✓			
Weight changes	✓						✓	✓		✓		✓	✓	✓	✓		✓	✓	✓			
Libido changes	✓						✓					✓	✓				✓	✓	✓			
Hirsutism	✓						✓					✓					✓		✓			
Scalp hair loss	✓						✓					✓					✓		✓			
Headache	✓						✓	✓		✓		✓		✓	✓		✓		✓			
Nervousness	✓						✓					✓					✓		✓			
Laboratory test interference	✓						✓					✓					✓		✓			
Jaundice	✓						✓					✓					✓		✓			
Blood pressure rise	✓						✓	✓				✓					✓		✓			
Chloasma												✓										
Miscellaneous reactions[b]	✓						✓					✓		✓			✓		✓			

31

TABLE 5 Continued.

ADVERSE REACTIONS, Continued	Ovulen						Norlestrin, Prolestrin					Ortho Novum, Novulon					Norinyl		Ovral, Anfertil			
	U.S.A.	Mexico	Central America	Ecuador,Colombia	Brazil	Argentina	U.S.A.	Mexico	Central America	Ecuador,Colombia	Argentina	U.S.A.	Mexico	Central America	Brazil	Argentina	U.S.A.	Mexico	U.S.A.	Ecuador,Colombia	Brazil	Argentina
NONE LISTED				X	X	X			X		X					X				X	X	X

aHigh dosage forms.

bMigraine, neuro-ocular lesions, cutaneous reactions, dizziness, fatigue, backache, emotional effects.

NOTE: Explanation of the sources of information in this table will be found on page ix.

4.

NONSTEROID ANTIARTHRITICS

For this section, three widely used drugs were chosen:

— phenylbutazone (marketed by CIBA-Geigy or Geigy as Butazolidin or Butazolidina, and by McKesson as Fenilbutazona MK)

— oxyphenbutazone (marketed by CIBA-Geigy or Geigy as Tandearil or Tanderil, and by McKesson as Oxifenbutazona MK)

— indomethacin (marketed by Merck Sharp & Dohme as Indocin and Indocid, and by McKesson as Indometacina MK)

CLINICAL BACKGROUND

Given the prevalence of arthritic diseases throughout the world, the need is evident for an agent more effective than aspirin, extremely safe, and relatively inexpensive to serve as the drug of choice in the treatment of arthritic conditions. It is equally evident that none of the three drugs considered in this study can meet such specifications. This is clearly emphasized in the United States, where standard reference works urge that phenylbutazone, oxyphenbutazone, and indomethacin should be prescribed in only a limited number of specified arthritic conditions, and only after other and safer therapy has proved to be inadequate. Strong warnings are presented against the use of these drugs by children and the elderly. Physicians and pharmacists are cautioned that their prescription for trivial or self-limiting conditions is unjustified, and that their use for prolonged periods in the treatment of chronic disease is particularly hazardous.

In the case of phenylbutazone, introduced in 1949, careless prescription for minor or chronic disease has been decried by many authorities. "Indiscriminate use of phenylbutazone in the therapy of trivial acute or chronic musculoskeletal disorders," it has been claimed, "can only be condemned."[1] A variety of authoritative sources in the United States stress the dangers associated with phenylbutazone and warn that it may produce life-threatening side effects.[2-4] Experts consulted by *The Medical Letter* considered phenylbutazone to be effective in relieving symptoms of ankylosing spondylitis and acute gout, but generally agreed that it should not be used for any chronic condition and that it is not a first-choice drug for any purpose.[5] *AMA Drug Evaluations* likewise notes that its usefulness is limited by its potential toxicity.[6]

In general, close medical supervision of the patient, including periodic blood examinations and dietary electrolyte restrictions, is considered to be mandatory. Use should be limited to short-term therapy, with an individual treatment period limited to one week. The patient should be warned to discontinue use of the drug and report immediately the development of any fever, rash, pruritus, jaundice, tarry stool, or weight increase. The drug is contraindicated in hypertensive patients, those with cardiac, renal, or hepatic dysfunction, and those with a history of peptic ulcer or any drug hypersensitivity.[7]

On the other hand, some experts feel that phenylbutazone may be used, with appropriate precautions, as the drug of choice in selected cases of acute gout and for extended therapy in selected cases of ankylosing spondylitis. Only specially qualified physicians, they indicate, should undertake such therapy.[8]

Goodman and Gilman state that some type of adverse reaction is seen in from 10 to 45 percent of all patients. Some of these reactions may appear to be of minor significance, but there are others, including development or reactivation of peptic ulcer, with hemorrhage or even perforation; ulcerative stomatitis; hepatitis; aplastic anemia; leukopenia; agranulocytosis; and thrombocytopenia. There have been reports of deaths, especially from aplastic anemia and agranulocytosis.[9]

Essentially the same information has been presented on oxyphenbutazone, a hydroxy analog and one of the major metabolic conversion products of phenylbutazone.[10] Physicians are urged to conduct repeated blood studies, but they are warned that even such studies may not make it possible to forestall unpredictable and sometimes fatal aplastic anemia and other serious reactions.

A similar situation exists in the case of indomethacin. While some early published accounts described its introduction as a "breakthrough" in the treatment of various types of arthritis, others reported it to be little if any more effective than aspirin. Thus, a survey conducted for the American Rheumatism Association failed to demonstrate any substantial benefit of the drug in comparison with a placebo.[11] One worker said, "There is no clear reason for preferring this drug over aspirin in treating rheumatoid arthritis. . . . The drug has severe side effects and should be used with caution."[12] From a Boston study comparing indomethacin with aspirin, it was concluded, "Neither drug has a subjective advantage or superiority as determined by measurement of grip strength, sedimentation rate, and number of tender and swollen joints."[13]

In 1966, shortly after Merck introduced its Indocin in the United States, FDA held that the labeling of the product was so misleading that it had been prescribed irrationally for children, some of whom died. The description of contraindications, FDA representatives said, was worded in such a way that a physician would not be informed of known hazards to children.[14] Upon FDA insistence, Merck changed the label to include the strong warning that indomethacin is flatly contraindicated for use in children under the age of fourteen.

During 1968, the development of the drug was examined in several Senate hearings, and its promotion by Merck was sharply criticized both by FDA officials and by private physicians as being seriously inadequate.[15]

As is the case with phenylbutazone and oxyphenbutazone, indomethacin is generally not considered to be the drug of choice for any condition because of its toxicity.[16] Its side effects seriously limit its use for extended periods. Even at usual therapeutic dosage levels, approximately 35 to 40 percent of patients experience untoward effects, and about 20 percent must discontinue its use. Some of these adverse reactions may be of minor importance, but others may have serious or fatal effects on the gastrointestinal tract, the central nervous system, the liver, and the blood.[17]

LABELING

Phenylbutazone

Both the phenylbutazone product and an "alka" product combining phenylbutazone with an antacid are listed in some countries. In most instances, the indications, contraindications and warnings, and adverse reactions are considered to be essentially the same for the two.

In the case of CIBA-Geigy's Butazolidin, United States physicians are told emphatically that it should not be considered to be a simple analgesic or administered casually. It has limited indications, usually severe forms of certain specified arthritic conditions. It carries the risk of causing stomach or duodenal ulcer, sometimes with perforation, and a serious or fatal blood dyscrasia. It is contraindicated in children and in senile patients. Treatment should be generally limited to a brief period, especially in the elderly (Table 6).

In striking contrast, Latin American physicians are advised that this product, along with McKesson's Fenilbutazona MK, is useful not only in serious arthritic diseases but also in a wide variety of conditions marked by fever, pain, and inflamation. The "alka" form is described as "especially indicated for patients with sensitive stomachs and for prolonged treatments, as well as in infancy, adolescence, and advanced age." In some countries, no contraindications, warnings, or adverse reactions are mentioned.

Oxyphenbutazone

In the United States, the indications for oxyphenbutazone—marketed under the name of Tandearil—are essentially the same as those for phenylbutazone, except that oxyphenbutazone is said to be indicated also for severe forms of a variety of local inflammatory conditions. (See Table 7.) It is not indicated, however, for the treatment of trivial conditions, and many of the disorders for which it has reportedly been found useful must be considered experimental indications pending further evaluation.

In Latin America, the indications for both CIBA-Geigy's Tanderil and McKesson's Oxyfenbutazona MK are far broader than those published in the United States, including bronchitis, tonsillitis, laryngitis, otitis, and sinisitis. Contraindications and warnings are minimized, and many adverse reactions—some of them serious or potentially fatal—are not disclosed.

Indomethacin

In the United States, Merck's Indocin is described as indicated in only four conditions: rheumatoid arthritis, ankylosing spondylitis, gout, and degenerative joint diseases of the hip (Table 8). The product marketed under the name of Indocid in Mexico, Central America, Colombia, Ecuador, Brazil, and Argentina is described not only for these four conditions but also for numerous others: acute musculoskeletal disorders such as tendinitis, synovitis, tenosynovitis, capsulitis of the shoulder joint, bursitis, lumbago, and osteoarthritis, and the relief of pain, inflammation, trismus, and edema following dental surgery and other surgical procedures. In Mexico, Central America, Colombia, and Ecuador, it is also described as indicated for the control of "fever" as a short-term adjunct to specific treatment.

A similar product, Indometacina MK, marketed by McKesson in Colombia and Ecuador, is recommended also for osteoarthritis and such acute musculoskeletal conditions as bursitis and tendinitis. For Merck's Indocid, there is substantial disclosure of hazards in the descriptions published in Mexico, Central America, Colombia, Ecuador, and Brazil. But for Indocid in Argentina and McKesson's Indometacina MK in Colombia and Ecuador, no hazards are disclosed.

TABLE 6. *Information given on:*

PHENYLBUTAZONE

marketed as BUTAZOLIDIN, BUTAZOLIDINA (CIBA-Geigy or Geigy), FENIL-
BUTAZONA MK (McKesson).

	CIBA-Geigy						McKesson	
	U.S.A.	Mexico	Central America	Ecuador, Colombia	Brazil	Argentina	Central America	Ecuador, Colombia
INDICATIONS FOR USE:								
Gout	√	√	√	√	√	√	√	
Rheumatoid arthritis	√	√	√	√	√		√	
Rheumatoid spondylitis	√							
Osteoarthritis	√							
Psoriatic arthritis	√	√		√			√	
Acute superficial thrombophlebitis	√	√	√	√	√	√	√	
Painful shoulder (peritendinitis, capsulitis, acute arthritis of that joint)	√							
Bursitis	√		√					
Rheumatic fever		√	√	√				
Bechterew's disease		√		√				
Ankylopoietic spondylarthritis		√	√					
Spondylosis		√	√	√			√	
Arthrosis		√	√	√			√	
All forms of fibrositis (tendinitis, peritendinitis)		√	√	√			√	
Scapulohumeral periarthritis		√	√					
Neuritis		√		√				
Spondylarthrosis			√					
Discopathies		√	√	√			√	
Coxal periarthritis			√					
Tendoperiostitis			√					
Humeral epicondylitis			√					
Myositis			√					
Myalgia			√					
Rheumatism of subcutaneous connective tissue			√					

TABLE 6 Continued.

	CIBA-Geigy						McKesson	
	U.S.A.	Mexico	Central America	Ecuador,Colombia	Brazil	Argentina	Central America	Ecuador,Colombia
INDICATIONS FOR USE, Continued								
Symptomatic treatment of Hodgkin's disease, other malignancies			✓			✓		
Miscellaneous processes with fever and pain			✓					
Progressive chronic polyarthritis							✓	
Ankylosing spondylarthritis							✓	
Periarthritis				✓			✓	
Acute polyarticular rheumatism					✓			
Acute general rheumatic process, acute general infections, local inflammatory processes					✓a			
Chronic rheumatic disorders					✓	✓		
"Anti-inflammatory, antirheumatic agent"								✓
CONTRAINDICATIONS AND WARNINGS:								
Warn patient of signs of blood dyscrasia	✓							
Short-term use in elderly	✓b							
Caution in elderly						✓		
Caution in pregnancy, nursing mothers	✓							
Contraindicated in senile patients	✓							
Contraindicated in children 14 or less	✓							
Caution if gastrointestinal inflammation or ulceration	✓c	✓	✓	✓	✓	✓	✓	
Contraindicated if severe, recurrent, or persistent dyspepsia	✓							
Caution if drug allergies	✓c						✓	
Caution if blood dyscrasias	✓c	✓	✓	✓	✓			
Caution if renal, hepatic, cardiac dysfunction	✓c	✓	✓			✓	✓	
Caution if hypertension	✓c						✓	
Contraindicated if thyroid disease, salivary gland enlargement or								

TABLE 6 Continued.

	U.S.A.	Mexico	Central America	Ecuador, Colombia	Brazil	Argentina	Central America	Ecuador, Colombia
			CIBA-Geigy				McKesson	
CONTRAINDICATIONS AND WARNINGS, Continued								
stomatitis due to drug, polymyalgia rheumatica, temporal periarteritis	✓							
Caution if systemic edema	✓c,d				✓		✓	
Contraindicated in patients on long-term anticoagulant therapy or receiving concurrent therapy with other potent chemotherapeutic agents	✓		✓					
Complete blood study every 1-2 weeks	✓							
Monitor blood picture						✓	✓	
Oliguria, insomnia		✓						
Hemorrhagic diathesis			✓	✓				
Hypersensitivity to pyrazolones			✓	✓				
Caution with cutaneous reactions						✓		
NONE LISTED								X
ADVERSE REACTIONS:								
Gastrointestinal ulceration, with perforation and hemorrhage	✓							
Reactivation of duodenal ulcers	✓					✓		
Gastric intolerance	✓			✓				
Gastritis	✓	✓						
Ulceration and perforation of large bowel	✓							
Nausea and vomiting	✓	✓						
Constipation or diarrhea	✓	✓						
Serious or fatal blood dyscrasias (agranulocytosis, aplastic anemia, hemolytic anemia, leukemia, etc.)	✓							
Moderate blood dyscrasias						✓		
Serious or fatal hepatitis	✓							

TABLE 6 Continued.

	CIBA-Geigy						McKesson	
	U.S.A.	Mexico	Central America	Ecuador, Colombia	Brazil	Argentina	Central America	Ecuador, Colombia
ADVERSE REACTIONS, Continued								
Allergic reactions (Stevens-Johnson syndrome, Lyell's syndrome, anaphylactic shock, etc.)	√							
Dermatologic reactions	√							
Urticaria	√	√						
Allergic dermatoses	√			√				
Fluid and electrolyte disturbances	√				√			
Edema	√	√						
Renal reactions (proteinuria, hematuria, acute tubular necrosis, etc.)	√							
Cardiovascular reactions (cardiac decompensation, hypertension, pericarditis, etc.)	√							
Ocular reactions (optic neuritis, blurred vision, retinal hemorrhage, etc.)	√							
Otic reactions (hearing loss)	√							
Hyperglycemia, thyroid hyperplasia, toxic goiter, etc.	√							
Agitation, confusional states, lethargy	√							
NONE LISTED			X			X	X	X

aSymptomatic treatment.

bOne week maximum therapy if possible.

cContraindicated if history or symptoms of condition.

dDiscontinue drug if edema appears.

NOTE: Explanation of the sources of information in this table will be found on page ix.

TABLE 7. *Information given on:*

OXYPHENBUTAZONE

marketed as TANDEARIL, TANDERIL (CIBA-Geigy or Geigy), OXIFENBU-TAZONA MK (McKesson).

	CIBA-Geigy						McKesson	
	U.S.A.	Mexico	Central America	Ecuador, Colombia	Brazil	Argentina	Central America	Ecuador, Colombia
INDICATIONS FOR USE:								
Rheumatoid arthritis	✓		✓					
Gout, rheumatoid spondylitis, osteo-arthritis, psoriatic arthritis, painful shoulder (peritendinitis, capsulitis, bursitis, acute arthritis of that joint)	✓							
Inflammatory rheumatism, rheumatic fever, ankylopoietic spondylitis, arthrosis, spondylosis, spondyl-arthrosis, extra-articular rheumatism (myalgia, lumbago, bursitis, tendovaginitis)			✓					
All forms of inflammatory and degenerative rheumatism				✓				
Tendovaginitis, bursitis, myositis, etc.		✓	✓				✓	✓
Acute superficial thrombophlebitis	✓	✓	✓				✓	✓
Neuritis		✓					✓	✓
Severe form of various local inflammatory conditions	✓							
Adjunct to chemotherapy in various inflammatory infectious diseases		✓	✓	✓	✓	✓	✓	✓
Post-traumatic inflammation and tumefaction (dislocations, distortions, contusions, fractures, etc.)		✓	✓				✓	✓
Inflammation of blood vessels and lymphatics				✓		✓		
Pre- and postsurgically in various gynecological, ophthalmological, otorhinolaryngological, urological, and other procedures		✓	✓			✓	✓	

TABLE 7 Continued.

		CIBA-Geigy					McKesson	
	U.S.A.	Mexico	Central America	Ecuador, Colombia	Brazil	Argentina	Central America	Ecuador, Colombia
INDICATIONS FOR USE, Continued								
Inflammation in dental abscesses, extraction, surgery, etc.		✓						
Inflammation of pelvic organs		✓	✓			✓	✓	✓
Post-traumatic tumefaction and inflammatory processes			✓	✓		✓	✓	
Inflammation in ophthalmology		✓		✓				
Local and generalized inflammatory processes					✓			
Prophylaxis and treatment of concomitant local and general phenomena related to radiotherapy of malignant tumors			✓	✓				
"Anti-inflammatory, analgesic agent"							✓	✓
CONTRAINDICATIONS AND WARNINGS:								
Warn patient of signs of blood dyscrasia	✓							
Short-term use in elderly	✓[a]							
Caution in pregnancy, nursing mothers	✓							
Caution in senile patients	✓							
Contraindicated in children 14 or less	✓							
Caution if gastrointestinal inflammation or ulceration	✓[b]	✓	✓	✓	✓	✓	✓	
Contraindicated if severe, recurrent, or persistent dyspepsia	✓							
Caution if drug allergies	✓[b]							
Caution if blood dyscrasias	✓[b]	✓	✓	✓	✓			
Caution if renal, hepatic, cardiac dysfunction	✓[b]	✓	✓	✓	✓	✓	✓	
Caution if hypertension	✓[b]							
Contraindicated if thyroid disease, salivary gland enlargement or stomatitis due to drug, polymyalgia rheumatica, temporal periarteritis	✓							

TABLE 7 Continued.

	CIBA-Geigy						McKesson	
	U.S.A.	Mexico	Central America	Ecuador, Colombia	Brazil	Argentina	Central America	Ecuador, Colombia
CONTRAINDICATIONS AND WARNINGS, Continued								
Caution if systemic edema	✓b,c							
Contraindicated in patients on long-term anticoagulant therapy or receiving concurrent therapy with other potent chemotherapeutic agents	✓							
Complete blood study every 1-2 weeks	✓							
Hemorrhagic diathesis		✓	✓	✓	✓	✓		
Hypersensitivity to pyrazolones		✓	✓	✓	✓	✓		
Hepatitis, nephritis, glomerulonephritis		✓		✓				
NONE LISTED								X
ADVERSE REACTIONS:								
Gastrointestinal ulceration with perforation and hemorrhage	✓							
Reactivation of duodenal ulcers	✓							
Gastric intolerance	✓	✓		✓				
Gastritis	✓							
Ulceration and perforation of large bowel	✓							
Nausea and vomiting	✓							
Constipation or diarrhea	✓							
Serious or fatal blood dyscrasias (agranulocytosis, aplastic anemia, hemolytic anemia, leukemia, etc.)	✓	✓						
Serious or fatal hepatitis	✓							
Allergic reactions (Stevens-Johnson syndrome, Lyell's syndrome, anaphylactic shock, etc.)	✓							
Dermatological reactions	✓	✓						
Urticaria	✓	✓						
Allergic dermatoses	✓	✓						
Fluid and electrolyte disturbances	✓							

TABLE 7 Continued.

| | U.S.A. | Mexico | CIBA-Geigy | | | | McKesson | |
			Central America	Ecuador,Colombia	Brazil	Argentina	Central America	Ecuador,Colombia
ADVERSE REACTIONS, Continued								
Edema	√							
Renal reactions (proteinuria, hematuria, acute tubular necrosis, etc.)	√							
Cardiovascular reactions (cardiac decompensation, hypertension, pericarditis, etc.)	√							
Ocular reactions (optic neuritis, blurred vision, retinal hemorrhage, etc.)	√							
Otic reactions (hearing loss)	√							
Hyperglycemia, thyroid hyperplasia, toxic goiter, etc.	√							
Agitation, confusional states, lethargy	√							
Stomatitis		√						
Labial herpes		√						
NONE LISTED			X		X	X	X	X

aOne week maximum therapy if possible.

bContraindicated if history or symptoms of condition.

cDiscontinue if edema appears.

NOTE: Explanation of the sources of information in this table will be found on page ix.

GOSHEN COLLEGE LIBRARY
GOSHEN, INDIANA

TABLE 8. *Information given on:*

INDOMETHACIN

marketed as INDOCIN, INDOCID (Merck Sharp & Dohme), INDOMETACINA MK (McKesson).

	Merck							McKesson
	U.S.A.	Mexico	Central America	Ecuador, Colombia	Brazil	Argentina		Ecuador, Colombia
INDICATIONS FOR USE:								
Rheumatoid arthritis	√a	√b	√	√b	√b	√		√
Osteoarthritis, degenerative disease of hip	√c	√	√	√	√	√		√
Gout	√d	√	√	√	√	√		√
Adjunct to steroid therapy in severe forms of rheumatoid arthritis	√e							
Ankylosing spondylitis		√	√	√	√			
Rheumatoid spondylitis						√		√
Musculoskeletal diseases		√	√f	√f	√f	√f		√f
Fever		√	√g	√g	√g			
Pain in dental ailments		√				√		
Postsurgical inflammation, trismus, edema		√	√h	√i	√h	√		
Lumbago			√	√	√			
CONTRAINDICATIONS AND WARNINGS:								
Contraindicated in children, pregnant women, nursing mothers	√	√	√	√	√			
Contraindicated in patients with history of recurrent gastrointestinal lesions or active gastrointestinal lesions	√	√	√	√	√			
Contraindicated in patients allergic to aspirin or indomethacin	√	√	√	√j	√			
Caution in elderly	√	√	√	√	√			
Be alert for any signs of possible gastrointestinal reaction	√	√		√	√			
Stop therapy if gastrointestinal bleeding occurs		√	√	√	√			

TABLE 8 Continued.

	U.S.A.	Mexico	Central America	Ecuador, Colombia	Brazil	Argentina		Ecuador, Colombia
			Merck					**McKesson**
CONTRAINDICATIONS AND WARNINGS, Continued								
Be alert for any ocular effects (corneal deposits, retinal disturbances)	✓	✓		✓	✓			
Periodic ophthalmologic examination desirable in prolonged therapy	✓	✓	✓	✓	✓			
May aggravate psychiatric disturbances, epilepsy, parkinsonism	✓	✓	✓	✓	✓			
Caution in activities requiring mental alertness	✓	✓k	✓k	✓k	✓k			
Stop therapy if headache persists despite dosage reduction	✓	✓	✓	✓	✓			
May mask signs and symptoms of infection	✓	✓		✓	✓			
Caution in presence of infection			✓		✓			
Conduct blood studies if hematological reactions suspected	✓	✓						
Be alert for unexpected manifestations of sensitivity			✓	✓	✓	✓		
NONE LISTED						X		X
ADVERSE REACTIONS:								
Gastrointestinal ulceration, including perforation and hemorrhage of esophagus, stomach, small bowel	✓l	✓l		✓l	✓l			
Perforation of preexisting sigmoid lesions; gastrointestinal bleeding, increased pain in ulcerative colitis, regional ileitis, nausea, vomiting, etc.	✓	✓		✓	✓			
Gastrointestinal disorders			✓					
Corneal deposits, retinal disturbances, blurring of vision	✓	✓		✓	✓			
Toxic hepatitis, jaundice	✓	✓		✓	✓			

TABLE 8 Continued.

ADVERSE REACTIONS, Continued	Merck							McKesson
	U.S.A.	Mexico	Central America	Ecuador, Colombia	Brazil	Argentina		Ecuador, Colombia
Aplastic anemia, hemolytic anemia, bone marrow depression, agranulocytosis, leukopenia, etc.	✓	✓		✓	✓			
Hypersensitivity reactions (acute respiratory distress, angiitis, pruritus, urticaria, etc.)	✓	✓		✓	✓			
Deafness, tinnitus	✓	✓		✓	✓			
Psychic disturbances, psychotic episodes, depersonalization, peripheral neuropathy, coma, convulsions, etc.	✓	✓		✓	✓			
Dizziness, headache	✓	✓	✓	✓	✓			
Edema	✓	✓		✓	✓			
Elevation of blood pressure	✓	✓		✓	✓			
Dermatologic reactions	✓	✓		✓	✓			
Stomatitis	✓	✓		✓	✓			
Hyperglycemia, glycosuria, etc.	✓	✓		✓	✓			
NONE LISTED						X		X

[a]In moderate to severe forms, including acute flares of chronic disease.

[b]In active states of disease.

[c]In moderate to severe forms.

[d]Effective in acute gouty arthritis in selected patients.

[e]May allow reduction of steroid dosage.

[f]Including bursitis, tendinitis, synovitis, tenosynovitis, capsulitis of shoulder joint.

[g]As short-term adjunct to specific therapy.

[h]Following dental surgery.

[i]Following dental and orthopedic surgery.

[j]Caution if concomitant treatment with steroids and salicylates.

[k]If patient experiences vertigo, should not operate motor vehicle.

[l]Fatal reactions reported.

NOTE: Explanation of the sources of information in this table will be found on page ix.

5.

STEROID HORMONES

In this section, attention is directed toward five important steroid hormone products:

— prednisone (marketed by Schering as Meticorten)

— betamethasone (marketed by Schering and by Essex as Celestone)

— triamcinolone (marketed by Lederle as Aristocort and Ledercort)

— methylprednisolone (marketed by Upjohn as Medrol)

— stanozolol (marketed by Winthrop as Winstrol)

The first four are usually classified as corticosteroids, used in the treatment of inflammatory conditions, allergic reactions, and other disorders, while stanozolol is an anabolic steroid.

CLINICAL BACKGROUND

Corticosteroids

During the past two decades, the corticosteroids—both the naturally occurring hormones and the many synthetic analogs now available— have won an accepted and reasonably well-defined role in medicine. While some have been applied effectively as substitution therapy in various types of adrenal insufficiency, others have proved useful in a variety of nonendocrine disorders. Included in the latter are such conditions as arthritis, rheumatic carditis, the nephrotic syndrome, systemic lupus erythematosus, bronchial asthma, a number of eye diseases, chronic ulcerative colitis, skin diseases, cerebral edema, leukemia, and shock.[1]

Unfortunately, it has been emphasized, these drugs in pharmacologic doses are "powerful drugs with slow cumulative toxic effects on all tissues, which may be inapparent until made manifest by a catastrophe."[2] Especially with long-term use, there may be peptic ulceration, intestinal perforation, gastritis, mental changes including psychotic episodes or paranoid states, muscular weakness, osteoporosis and vertebral fracture, facial rounding, and exacerbation of a preexisting diabetes. A particularly serious side effect is the reactivation of healed or latent tuberculosis. Under corticosteroid therapy, patients may be more susceptible to fungal, bacterial, and viral infections.[3]

The incidence of important undesired reactions has been reported by Nielsen et al., based on a study of approximately 300 patient-years of experience in 50 patients. Mental disturbances occurred in 24 percent, peptic ulcer in 18 percent, vertebral fractures in 6 percent, pneumonia in 14 percent, and death in 18 percent.[4]

While the corticosteroids have a marked anti-inflammatory effect, notably in arthritic disease, they control the manifestations of inflammation rather than the underlying disease process of tissue destruction and fibrosis. In rheumatoid arthritis, progressive joint destruction continues despite their use. As Williams and Becker have noted, "They are not a panacea for inflammatory disorders."[5] Others have stated, "Each pharmacologic agent has a 'price tag' which must be evaluated carefully before a therapeutic program is begun."[6]

Accordingly, it has been recommended that the corticosteroids should be used in pharmacologic (rather than physiologic) doses for prolonged periods only for patients with life-threatening conditions or with severe symptoms that cannot be satisfactorily controlled with less hazardous treatments. Except in urgent conditions, their long-term use is generally contraindicated in children, because of the possibility of growth suppression, and in patients with psychoses, severe neuroses, or convulsive disorders.[7]

Except for variations in sodium retention and potassium loss, there are few significant differences in the contraindications, warnings, and adverse reactions for the corticosteroids surveyed here.[8]

Anabolic Steroids

Heralded at first for their possible value in stimulating the absorption
of nutritive materials and transforming these into body tissues, the
synthetic anabolic steroids were proposed for use in patients recovering
from surgery, infections, burns, fractures, emaciating diseases, and
severe traumatic injuries. There appears to be no adequate evidence,
however, that they speed recovery. In the same way, hopes that these
agents would be of significant aid in the treatment of osteoporosis have
not been confirmed.[9]

Some investigators have proposed the use of anabolic steroids, with
their androgen effect, for the treatment of prepuberal children with
growth failure. Other authorities note that such therapy requires
careful consideration, since the expected benefits may not justify the
risks of precocious puberty in boys, virilism in girls, and premature
closure of epiphyses.[10, 11]

The use of these substances is contraindicated in pregnant women or
women who may become pregnant during the course of treatment,
male patients with carcinoma of the prostate or breast, patients with
nephrosis, and those patients with renal or cardiac disease who may be
predisposed to edema.[12]

The value of the anabolic steroids in increasing hemoglobin levels in
some patients with aplastic anemia appears to be well established.[13]

LABELING

The indications listed for the corticosteroid hormones discussed here
are generally similar. In the United States, these include a wide variety
of endocrine, rheumatic, allergic, and other disorders, all described in
considerable detail. In Latin America, the indications are given more
broadly and less specifically. In some Latin American countries, these
hormone products are recommended also for the treatment of
emphysema and pulmonary fibrosis (Table 9). Where the hazards of
each product are concerned, the differences are more striking.

Prednisone

In the United States, emphatic warnings are placed on the use of
Meticorten for prolonged periods in infants and children, pregnant

women, nursing mothers, and women in their childbearing years. Physicians are advised that long-term use may lead to suppression of growth in children and to such serious reactions as severe mental disturbances, peptic ulceration with bleeding and perforation, bone softening, fractures of the vertebrae, serious muscle damage, convulsions, glaucoma, vertigo, hypertension, reactivation of latent tuberculosis, and heightened susceptibility to a variety of fungal, viral, and bacterial infections.

For Meticorten, warnings are presented in Latin America for infections, peptic ulcer, emotional instability, and osteoporosis, but most of the other hazards are not mentioned.

Betamethasone

The contraindications and warnings listed for Celestone in Latin America, like those for Meticorten, cover some but not all those disclosed in the United States. So far as adverse reactions are concerned, only osteoporosis, psychic changes, and "typical corticosteroid reactions" are listed in Mexico. In Central America, Colombia, Ecuador, Brazil, and Argentina, no adverse reactions are listed.

Triamcinolone

For the Lederle product, some contraindications and warnings are presented in Mexico, Colombia, Ecuador, Brazil, and Argentina, but only a nonspecific warning is listed in Central America. In Mexico, only a few adverse reactions — the possible development of a Cushingoid state and the occurrence of insomnia, euphoria, and hirsutism — are mentioned. In Brazil, physicians are cautioned against the development of osteoporosis, peptic ulcer, and decreased carbohydrate tolerance. The descriptions in Central America, Colombia, and Ecuador include only "typical corticosteroid reactions." No adverse reactions are listed in Argentina.

Methylprednisolone

Only a few contraindications and warnings are noted in the description of Medrol in Mexico and Argentina. Mexican physicians are alerted to the possible occurrence of insomnia, euphoria, and hirsutism. No adverse reactions are listed in Argentina.

Stanozolol

In the case of Winthrop's anabolic steroid Winstrol, indications in the United States are limited mainly to some cases of aplastic anemia and as adjunctive therapy in selected cases of osteoporosis and pituitary dwarfism (Table 10). Latin American physicians, however, are told that the drug is indicated when an increase in weight or strength is desired, or when there is need for an increase in appetite. In some Latin American countries, it is described broadly as useful in the treatment of cirrhosis and chronic hepatitis, preoperative and postoperative care, convalescence, and geriatrics, and as supportive therapy in both chronic and acute illness. In the United States and some Latin American countries, the potential hazards — including growth-stunting in children, jaundice, premature sexual development in prepuberal males, testicular atrophy or impotence in older males, and hirsutism, deepening of the voice, and menstrual irregularities in females — are disclosed in detail. In other Latin American countries, notably Colombia and Ecuador, they are minimized or ignored.

TABLE 9. *Information given on:*

CORTICOSTEROIDS

Prednisone *marketed as* METICORTEN (Schering), Betamethasone *marketed as* CELESTONE (Schering and Essex), Triamcinolone *marketed as* ARISTOCORT, LEDERCORT (Lederle), Methylprednisolone *marketed as* MEDROL (Upjohn).

	Prednisone				Betamethasone						Triamcinolone						Methyl-prednisolone		
	U.S.A.	Mexico	Brazil	Argentina	U.S.A.	Mexico	Central America	Ecuador,Colombia	Brazil	Argentina	U.S.A.	Mexico	Central America	Ecuador,Colombia	Brazil	Argentina	U.S.A.	Mexico	Argentina
INDICATIONS FOR USE:																			
General	√a	√a	√a	√a	√a	√a	√a	√b	√a	√a	√a	√a	√a	√a	√a	√c	√a	√a	√a
Pulmonary emphysema		√				√	√		√				√	√	√		√d	√a	
Pulmonary fibrosis		√				√	√		√	√			√	√	√		√d		
Ulcerative colitis						√	√										√d,e	√	√
Regional enteritis																	√d,e		
Intractable sprue																	√d,e		
Liver cirrhosis												√					√d,f		
Insect bites												√							
CONTRAINDICATIONS AND WARNINGS:																			
Systemic fungal infection					√						√	√					√		
May mask signs of infection					√				√		√				√		√		

TABLE 9 Continued.

	Prednisone				Betamethasone						Triamcinolone						Methyl-prednisolone		
CONTRAINDICATIONS AND WARNINGS, Continued	U.S.A.	Mexico	Brazil	Argentina	U.S.A.	Mexico	Central America	Ecuador, Colombia	Brazil	Argentina	U.S.A.	Mexico	Central America	Ecuador, Colombia	Brazil	Argentina	U.S.A.	Mexico	Argentina
Latent or active tuberculosis	✓	✓	✓	✓	✓	✓		✓	✓	✓	✓	✓		✓	✓	✓	✓	✓	✓
Acute or chronic infection	✓	✓	✓		✓	✓			✓	✓	✓				✓		✓		✓
Caution with immunizations	✓				✓						✓						✓		
Ocular herpes simplex	✓	✓	✓	✓	✓	✓		✓	✓	✓	✓	✓			✓	✓	✓	✓	✓
Active or latent peptic ulcer	✓	✓	✓		✓	✓		✓	✓	✓	✓	✓			✓	✓	✓	✓	✓
Nonspecific ulcerative colitis9	✓				✓						✓						✓		
Emotional instability	✓	✓	✓	✓	✓	✓		✓	✓	✓	✓	✓			✓	✓	✓	✓	✓
Renal insufficiency	✓	✓			✓	✓			✓	✓	✓				✓		✓	✓	
Osteoporosis	✓		✓	✓	✓				✓	✓	✓	✓			✓		✓		
Diabetes	✓		✓		✓				✓		✓				✓		✓		
Hypertension	✓				✓	✓			✓		✓				✓		✓	✓	
Cardiovascular disease									✓						✓		✓	✓	
Caution in pregnant, nursing women	✓		✓		✓						✓				✓		✓		
Caution in infants and children	✓		✓		✓						✓				✓		✓		
"Others common to corticosteroids"					✓	✓							✓	✓					

TABLE 9 Continued.

ADVERSE REACTIONS:	Prednisone				Betamethasone						Triamcinolone						Methyl-prednisolone		
	U.S.A.	Mexico	Brazil	Argentina	U.S.A.	Mexico	Central America	Ecuador, Colombia	Brazil	Argentina	U.S.A.	Mexico	Central America	Ecuador, Colombia	Brazil	Argentina	U.S.A.	Mexico	Argentina
CONTRAINDICATIONS AND WARNINGS, Continued																			
NONE LISTED							X												
ADVERSE REACTIONS:																			
Fluid and electrolyte disturbances	✓				✓						✓						✓		
Congestive heart failure	✓				✓						✓						✓		
Hypertension	✓				✓						✓				✓		✓		
Muscle weakness	✓				✓						✓				✓		✓		
Osteoporosis	✓	✓			✓	✓					✓						✓		
Vertebral compression fractures	✓				✓						✓						✓		
Peptic ulcer with perforation and hemorrhage															✓				
Impaired wound healing	✓				✓						✓						✓		
Convulsions	✓				✓						✓						✓		
Vertigo	✓				✓						✓						✓		
Headache	✓				✓						✓						✓		

56

TABLE 9 Continued.

	Prednisone				Betamethasone[a]						Triamcinolone						Methyl-prednisolone		
	U.S.A.	Mexico	Brazil	Argentina	U.S.A.	Mexico	Central America	Ecuador, Colombia	Brazil	Argentina	U.S.A.	Mexico	Central America	Ecuador, Colombia	Brazil	Argentina	U.S.A.	Mexico	Argentina
ADVERSE REACTIONS, Continued																			
Menstrual irregularities	✓				✓						✓	✓			✓		✓		
Cushingoid state	✓				✓						✓						✓		
Suppression of growth in children	✓	✓			✓						✓				✓		✓		
Decreased carbohydrate tolerance	✓				✓						✓						✓		
Manifestations of latent diabetes	✓				✓						✓						✓		
Subcapsular cataracts	✓				✓						✓						✓		
Glaucoma, etc.	✓	✓			✓						✓						✓		
Psychic changes	✓	✓	✓		✓	✓					✓	✓					✓	✓	
Insomnia, euphoria, hirsutism					✓	✓					✓	✓	✓	✓			✓	✓	
"Typical corticosteroid reactions"																			
NONE LISTED				X			X	X	X	X						X			X

a Wide variety of endocrine, rheumatic, collagen, dermatologic, allergic, ophthalmic, respiratory, hematologic, neoplastic, edematous, and other disorders.

b Indicated as "anti-inflammatory, antirheumatic, and antiallergic agent."

57

TABLE 9 Continued.

[c]Indicated for "anti-inflammatory, hormonal, and metabolic effects—in all disorders subject to corticotherapy."

[d]"Probably effective."

[e]Use as adjunct.

[f]To tide patient over critical period of disease.

[g]Caution if probability of impending perforation.

NOTE: Explanation of the sources of information in this table will be found on page ix.

TABLE 10. *Information given on:*

STANOZOLOL
marketed as WINSTROL (Winthrop).

	U.S.A.	Mexico	Central America	Ecuador, Colombia	Brazil	Argentina
INDICATIONS FOR USE:						
Protein synthesis increase, anabolic effect	✓	✓	✓	✓	✓	
Increase hemoglobin in aplastic anemia	✓					
Senile or postmenopausal osteoporosis, as adjunct	✓a					✓
Pituitary dwarfism	✓					
Weight increase		✓	✓	✓	✓	✓
Anorexia		✓	✓	✓	✓	✓
Strength increase		✓	✓	✓	✓	
Cirrhosis, chronic hepatitis		✓	✓	✓	✓	
Preoperative, postoperative, convalescent care		✓	✓	✓	✓	✓
Supportive treatment, acute and chronic illness		✓	✓	✓		
Tonic action in elderly					✓	✓
Gastrointestinal diseases						✓
Burns						✓
Renal disorders						✓
CONTRAINDICATIONS AND WARNINGS:						
Prostate carcinoma	✓	✓	✓		✓	✓
Breast carcinoma	✓					
Benign prostate hypertrophy	✓					
Pregnancy	✓	✓	✓		✓	✓
Cardiac disease	✓	✓	✓		✓	
Renal disease, nephrosis	✓	✓	✓		✓	
Hepatic disease	✓		✓		✓	
Edema	✓		✓			
Caution in coronary artery disease	✓		✓			
Caution in infants and children, check bone x-rays	✓	✓	✓		✓	
Laboratory test interference	✓		✓		✓	
Caution in patients on anticoagulant therapy	✓					
NONE LISTED				X		

TABLE 10 Continued.

	U.S.A.	Mexico	Central America	Ecuador, Colombia	Brazil	Argentina
ADVERSE REACTIONS:						
Nausea, vomiting, diarrhea	✓					
Excitation, insomnia, chills	✓					
Changes in libido	✓					
Acne	✓					
Premature closing of epiphyses in children	✓	✓			✓	
Jaundice, rarely with hepatic necrosis and death	✓					
Phallic enlargement in prepuberal males	✓				✓	
Inhibition of testicular function, impotence, gynecomastia, priapism, etc. in postpuberal males	✓					
Hirsutism, voice deepening in females	✓b	✓	✓c		✓c	✓c
Male pattern baldness, clitoral enlargement in females	✓b					
Menstrual irregularities	✓	✓	✓		✓	✓
NONE LISTED				X		

a"Probably effective."

bUsually irreversible even after prompt suspension of treatment.

cReversible by reducing dosage or suspending treatment.

NOTE: Explanation of the sources of information in this table will be found on page ix.

6.

ANTIPSYCHOTIC TRANQUILIZERS

Three widely used "major" or antipsychotic tranquilizers were selected for study. These were:

—chlorpromazine (marketed in the United States as Thorazine by Smith Kline & French, in Mexico as Largactil by Rhône-Poulenc—Rhodia Mexicana, in Central America as Largactil by Specia—Société Parisienne d'Expansion Chimique, in Brazil as Amplictil by Rhodia, and in Argentina as Ampliactil by Rhodia Argentina)

—thioridazine (marketed as Mellaril, Melleril, and Meleril by Sandoz)

—trifluoperazine (marketed as Stelazine by Smith Kline & French)

Clinical Background

In 1952, Charpentier in the laboratories of Rhône-Poulenc in Paris synthetized drug number 4560 RP, or chlorpromazine. A seemingly minor molecular modification of compounds investigated earlier as antihistamines, it was soon to be hailed as the first of the synthetic antipsychotic agents or "major" tranquilizers. In the next year, Courvoisier and her associates described a large number of actions— hence the brand name Largactil—manifested by the new substance.[1]

Currently chlorpromazine, thioridazine, trifluoperazine, and other antipsychotic phenothiazines are accepted as valuable in the treatment of acute and chronic schizophrenia, the manic phase of manic-depressive psychosis, and involutional, senile, organic, and toxic psychoses, with the exception of delirium tremens.[2]   Their use in such conditions has had a dramatic effect in the treatment of mental disease. In most of these applications, the benefits of the drugs apparently far outweigh their known hazards.

These agents may be of limited value in a few other conditions. In the treatment of neuroses and psychosomatic illnesses, however, the so-called antianxiety or "minor" tranquilizers generally appear to be preferred. The efficacy of the antipsychotic drugs in these less serious psychiatric illnesses has not been definitely established. In addition, more severe adverse reactions are generally associated with use of the antipsychotic drugs.[3]

Many investigators have reportedly found it difficult if not impossible to distinguish one of the commonly used antipsychotic phenothiazine compounds from another on the basis of efficacy.[4]

In recent years, special attention has been directed to such serious side effects as agranulocytosis, changes in cardiac function, a variety of neurological changes including parkinsonism-like states, and tardive dyskinesia.[5]

The seriousness of the problem of phenothiazine-induced tardive dyskinesia, once a matter of considerable dispute, has now been generally recognized.[6] This disorder is marked by involuntary movements affecting particularly the lips, tongue, hands, fingers, feet, and body posture. Speech may be seriously affected, the face distorted and subject to uncontrollable expressions. Sustained posture may become impossible.[7] A high incidence of this reaction has been noted especially in schizophrenic patients under long-term treatment with relatively large doses of phenothiazines.[8] In one review of 3,775 patients treated with phenothiazine derivatives, Ayd noted that 1,472, or 38.9 percent, developed extrapyramidal reactions. About 21.2 percent had akathisia, 15.4 percent had parkinsonism, and 2.3 percent had one form or another of dyskinesia.[9] A German survey of 1,600 psychiatric patients receiving long-term treatment with such tranquilizers revealed that about 27 percent of the women and 18 percent of the men showed toxic signs of chronic extrapyramidal hyperkinesia.[10] Greenblatt has reported that 30 percent of nursing-home patients treated with phenothiazines developed dyskinesia unrelated to chronic brain syndrome, length of stay in the home, or age of the patient.[11] In a recent review, Anderson and Kuehnle have stated: "The optimal goal is to avoid one unnecessary milligram for one unnecessary week. . . . Given our imperfect understanding of the long-term consequences of antipsychotic chemotherapy, the phenomenon of tardive dyskinesia is at present the most serious concern."[12]

In many victims, it has been reported, the disturbances become irreversible. No effective treatment for tardive dyskinesia is known.[13]

LABELING

Chlorpromazine

In the United States, Mexico, Central America and Argentina, the major indication described for this tranquilizer is management of the manifestations of psychic disorders. Also included among important uses are the control of nausea, vomiting, and intractable hiccups (Table 11). In Brazil, it is said to have a calming and tranquilizing action that "causes its use in the treatment of mental and emotional disturbances to be of inestimable value."

In addition, the chlorpromazine products in most of the other Latin American countries are listed as indicated in the treatment of neuroses, psychosomatic disorders, menstrual pain, and sleep disorders, and to prevent or control traumatic or postsurgical shock.

Through *PDR*, physicians in the United States are given a substantial list of contraindications and warnings concerning the use of Thorazine. Few such warnings are presented in Latin America. In Brazil, the sole warning appears to be the advice that during the initial days of treatment with the injectable form, especially in those with high or low blood pressure, patients should remain in a horizontal position for half an hour after the drug is administered.

As with contraindications and warnings, a long and detailed list of potential adverse reactions is included in *PDR*, and it is noted that some sudden deaths associated with use of the drug have been reported. Special emphasis is directed toward the appearance of tardive dyskinesia and various parkinsonism-like conditions, especially with the use of high doses. "Persistent tardive dyskinesia may appear after drug therapy has been discontinued," it is stated. "The symptoms are persistent and in some patients appear to be irreversible. There is no known effective treatment . . ."

In Mexico, only a few adverse reactions are mentioned. In Central America, Brazil, and Argentina, no such reactions are listed.

Thioridazine

In the United States, Mellaril is described as effective in the management of psychotic disorders, "probably" effective in neurotic depressive reaction and in agitated, hyperactive, disturbed children, and "possibly" effective in psychoneurosis and a few other states (Table 12). Latin American physicians are told that the drug is useful in a substantial number of conditions, including such pediatric problems as sleepwalking, nocturnal fears, nightmares, bed-wetting, insomnia, and inability to adapt in school.

In the United States, the numerous contraindications, warnings, and potential adverse reactions for Mellaril are essentially the same as those for chlorpromazine. A few such warnings and adverse effects are presented in Mexico. None are listed in Central America, Colombia, Ecuador, or Argentina.

Trifluoperazine

A low-dosage form of Stelazine is marketed in the United States, Mexico, Central America, Brazil, and Argentina. A high-dosage form is described in Mexico and Brazil.

As with the two other phenothiazine tranquilizers discussed in this chapter, the indications for Stelazine are limited in the United States and far more extensive in the Latin American countries. In Mexico and Brazil, the high-dosage form is described as useful in such conditions as chronic alcoholism and mental deficiency (Table 13).

Many of the same contraindications and warnings described in the United States are also given in Mexico, Central America, and Brazil. Physicians in Mexico, Central America, and Brazil are alerted to the possible occurrence of such adverse reactions as drowsiness, skin reactions, insomnia, and fatigue, but little emphasis is placed on such reactions as irreversible tardive dyskinesia, eye damage, and a life-threatening drop in blood pressure.

TABLE 11. *Information given on:*

CHLORPROMAZINE

marketed as THORAZINE (Smith Kline & French [U.S.A.]), LARGACTIL (Rhône-Poulenc–Rhodia Mexicana [Mexico], Specia–Société Parisienne d'Expansion Chimique [Central America]), AMPLICTIL (Rhodia [Brazil]), AMPLIACTIL (Rhodia Argentina [Argentina]).

	U.S.A.	Mexico	Central America	Brazil	Argentina
INDICATIONS FOR USE:					
Management of manifestations of psychic disorders	✓	✓	✓		✓
Control of nausea and vomiting	✓	✓	✓		✓
Control of manifestations of manic-depressive illness (manic phase)	✓	✓	✓		
Relief of intractable hiccups	✓	✓	✓		✓
Control of restlessness and apprehension prior to surgery	✓		✓		✓
Control of acute intermittent porphyria	✓				
Adjunct in treatment of tetanus	✓				
Reduction of agitation, tension, nausea, etc., in mild alcohol withdrawal	✓a				
Control of agitation, hyperactivity, aggressiveness in disturbed children	✓a				
Reduction of apprehension, suffering, etc., in cancer and severe pain	✓b				
Control of excessive anxiety, tension, agitation in neuroses	✓b				✓
Dystonias of neurovegetative system		✓	✓		✓
Resistant pruritus of endogenous origin		✓	✓		
Dysmenorrhea		✓	✓		
Psychosomatic disorders		✓			✓
Potentiation of anesthetics, analgesics, narcotics, etc.		✓	✓		✓
Obstetrical analgesia		✓	✓		
Eclampsia		✓	✓		✓
Prevention, treatment of traumatic and postsurgical shock		✓	✓		✓
Treatment of surgical hyperthermia		✓	✓		✓
Controlled hypotensive therapy		✓	✓		
Induced hypothermia or artificial hibernation		✓	✓		✓
Premedication for endoscopic examination		✓	✓		

TABLE 11 Continued.

	U.S.A.	Mexico	Central America	Brazil	Argentina
INDICATIONS FOR USE, Continued					
Toxic and neurotoxic states in nursing infants		✓	✓		
Various disorders accompanying severe infections, encephalitis, diverse neuralgias, convulsive manifestations in epilepsy, tetanus, etc.		✓	✓		
Agitation, acute psychomotor excitation		✓	✓		
Delirium tremens		✓			
Psychoneurosis		✓			
Senile dementia		✓			
Schizophrenia		✓	✓		
Psychosomatic ailments		✓			✓
Various hallucinatory confusional states		✓	✓		
Adjunct in treatment of sleep disorders		✓	✓		✓
Malignant syndromes of infectious diseases in children		✓			
Adjunct in treatment of severe toxic infections		✓			
Fitful coughing, acute laryngitis		✓			
Neurodermatitis		✓			
Pernicious malarial attacks		✓			
Neuralgias, sympathalgias, painful spasms		✓			
Coma caused by carbon dioxide intoxication, edema, etc.		✓			
Melancholia		✓			
"Calming and tranquilizing effect" in treatment of "mental and emotional disturbances"				✓	
Hypertension					✓
Convulsions					✓
Dyskinesias					✓
Complement to psychotherapy					✓
"Essential and symptomatic painful conditions"					✓
"Anguish"					✓
CONTRAINDICATIONS AND WARNINGS:					
Contraindicated in comatose states, presence of large amounts of central nervous system depressants (alcohol, barbiturates, etc.)	✓	✓	✓		✓

TABLE 11 Continued.

	U.S.A.	Mexico	Central America	Brazil	Argentina
CONTRAINDICATIONS AND WARNINGS, Continued					
Contraindicated in presence of bone marrow depression	✓	✓			
Caution in patients with hypersensitivity to any phenothiazine	✓				
Warn patients about activities requiring alertness	✓				
Use of alcohol should be avoided	✓				
Caution in patients using guanethidine and related antihypertensive products	✓				
Caution in pregnant women	✓				
Caution in patients with cardiovascular, hepatic disease	✓	✓			
Caution in patients with chronic respiratory disease (severe asthma, emphysema), acute respiratory infections	✓				
Can suppress cough reflex	✓c				
Can intensify and prolong action of such central nervous system depressants as anesthetics, barbiturates, and narcotics	✓	✓			
Caution in persons who will be exposed to extreme heat or organophosphorus insecticides, or are receiving atropine or related drugs	✓				
May mask signs of overdosage of toxic drugs	✓				
May obscure intestinal obstruction, brain tumor, etc.	✓				
For parenteral administration, patients should be recumbent for first injections			✓	✓	
Regular ophthalmic examination recommended in prolonged treatment			✓		
ADVERSE REACTIONS:					
Drowsiness	✓	✓			
Jaundice (rare, probably sensitivity reaction)	✓				
Agranulocytosis, eosinophilia, hemolytic anemia, etc. (rare)	✓				
Hypotensive effects	✓				
Electrocardiogram changes	✓				
Extrapyramidal parkinsonism-like reactions	✓				

TABLE 11 Continued.

	U.S.A.	Mexico	Central America	Brazil	Argentina
ADVERSE REACTIONS, Continued					
Dystonic reactions, hyperreflexia	✓				
Tardive dyskinesia	✓d				
Adverse behavioral effects, other central nervous system effects, cerebral edema, convulsive seizures	✓				
Allergic reactions	✓				
Photosensitivity	✓	✓			
Lactation, moderate breast engorgement, false-positive pregnancy test, amenorrhea, etc.	✓				
Hyperglycemia, hypoglycemia, glycosuria	✓				
Mouth dryness	✓	✓			
Nasal congestion	✓				
Constipation, adynamic ileus	✓	✓			
Urinary retention	✓				
Miosis, mydriasis	✓				
Ocular changes, hyperpyrexia, increases in appetite and weight, peripheral edema, systemic lupus erythematosus-like syndrome	✓				
Pallor, vertigo, headache, polyuria, lowering of body temperature, asthenia, prostration		✓			
With parenteral administration, orthostatic hypertension, tachycardia		✓			
NONE LISTED			X	X	X

a"Probably effective."

b"Possibly effective."

cFatalities reported from asphyxia.

dPersistent, sometimes irreversible; may appear during treatment or after therapy discontinued.

NOTE: Explanation of the sources of information in this table will be found on page ix.

TABLE 12. *Information given on:*

THIORIDAZINE

marketed as MELLARIL, MELLERIL, MELERIL (Sandoz).

	U.S.A.	Mexico	Central America	Ecuador, Colombia	Argentina
INDICATIONS FOR USE:					
Management of manifestations of psychotic disorders	✓				✓
Relief of symptoms of neurotic depressive reaction	✓a				✓
Control of moderate to severe agitation, hyperactivity, aggressiveness in disturbed children	✓a				
Alcohol withdrawal syndrome	✓b				
Intractable pain	✓b				
Psychoneurosis	✓b				✓
Senility	✓b				✓
States of anguish and emotional tension accompanied by psychosomatic disorders (cardiovascular, gastrointestinal)		✓	✓		✓
Insomnia		✓			
States of excitation, psychosis		✓			✓
Alcoholism cures		✓			
In children: sleepwalking, behavioral disorders (difficult children), nocturnal fears, enuresis		✓			
Agitated states, emotional tension, or anxiety states in all stages and of various causes			✓		
In children: behavioral disorders and hostility reactions, inability to adapt in school, insomnia, sleepwalking, nightmares, psychogenic anorexia, nocturnal enuresis, nail-biting			✓		
States of anxiety, tension, agitation, irritability, sleep disturbances, conduct disorders, psychosomatic alterations				✓	
In children: anxiety states, states of agitation, concentration difficulty, behavioral disturbances, emotional enuresis				✓	
Anxiety-tension, neurotic states					✓
Hyperexcitability, paranoid ideas, hallucinations, mild obsessive and anxiety neuroses					✓
Alcoholic delirium					✓

TABLE 12 Continued.

	U.S.A.	Mexico	Central America	Ecuador, Colombia	Argentina
CONTRAINDICATIONS AND WARNINGS:					
Contraindicated in severe central nervous system depression or comatose states from any cause, hypertensive or hypotensive heart disease of extreme degree	✓	✓			
Caution if hypersensitivity to any phenothiazine	✓				
Can potentiate central nervous system depressants (anesthetics, opiates, alcohol, etc.), atropine, phosphorus-containing insecticides	✓				
Caution in pregnant women	✓				
Warning of blood dyscrasias, convulsions, pigmentary retinopathy (diminution of visual acuity, etc.), orthostatic hypotension especially in women	✓				
Warning against exceeding recommended dosages	✓				
Caution with patients participating in activities requiring complete alertness	✓				
NONE LISTED			X	X	X
ADVERSE REACTIONS:					
Drowsiness, lethargy, somnolence	✓	✓			
Pseudoparkinsonism, other extrapyramidal symptoms, nocturnal confusion, hyperactivity, psychotic reactions, restlessness, headache	✓				
Mouth dryness, blurred vision, nausea, vomiting, diarrhea, pallor	✓				
Constipation, nasal stuffiness	✓	✓			
Breast engorgement, amenorrhea, peripheral edema	✓				
Galactorrhea, inhibition of ejaculation (diminished libido)	✓	✓			
Dermatitis, urticaria-like skin eruptions, other cutaneous reactions	✓				
Photosensitivity	✓	✓			
Electrocardiogram changes	✓				
Miosis, anorexia, paralytic ileus[c]	✓				

TABLE 12 Continued.

	U.S.A.	Mexico	Central America	Ecuador, Colombia	Argentina
ADVERSE REACTIONS, Continued					
Agranulocytosis, thrombocytopenia, anemia, aplastic anemia, pancytopenia[c]	✓				
Allergic reactions (fever, laryngeal edema, angio-neurotic edema, asthma)[c]	✓				
Cardiovascular effects (cardiac arrest)[c]	✓				
Akathisia, agitation, motor restlessness, dystonia reactions, trismus, torticollis, other extrapyramidal symptoms[c]	✓				
Menstrual irregularities, weight gain, false pregnancy tests, other endocrine disturbances[c]	✓				
Urinary retention, incontinence[c]	✓				
Hyperpyrexia, behavioral effects (excitement, bizarre dreams, aggravation of psychosis, toxic confusional states)[c]	✓				
Progressive pigmentation of areas of skin or conjunctiva and/or accompanied by discoloration of exposed sclera and cornea[c]	✓				
Opacities of anterior lens and cornea[c]	✓				
Cutaneous reactions[c]	✓				
NONE LISTED			X	X	X

[a]"Probably effective" (use in neurotic depressive reaction later reclassified as "effective").

[b]"Possibly effective."

[c]Have occurred with one or more phenothiazine products.

NOTE: Explanation of the sources of information in this table will be found on page ix.

TABLE 13. *Information given on:*

TRIFLUOPERAZINE

marketed as STELAZINE (Smith Kline & French).

	1-2mg					5-10mg	
	U.S.A.	Mexico	Central America	Brazil	Argentina	Mexico	Brazil
INDICATIONS FOR USE:							
Management of manifestations of psychotic disorders	✓						
Control of excessive anxiety, tension, and agitation as seen in neuroses or associated with somatic conditions	✓[a]						
Mental and emotional disorders		✓	✓				
Control of excessive anxiety, whether expressed as tension and agitation or as apathy and indifference		✓	✓	✓			
Relief of anxiety that accompanies or causes somatic disorders		✓	✓	✓			
Nausea and vomiting of various causes		✓	✓	✓	✓		
Anxiety and tension states, behavioral disorders, prepsychotic states					✓		
Rapid response in psychotic states such as acute and chronic schizophrenia, manic-depressive psychosis, involutional psychosis, psychosis as result of organic cerebral damage, toxic psychosis, chronic alcoholism, and mental deficiency						✓	✓
CONTRAINDICATIONS AND WARNINGS:							
Contraindicated in comatose states	✓	✓	✓	✓	✓	✓	
Contraindicated in greatly depressed states caused by central nervous system depressants	✓	✓	✓	✓		✓	
Contraindicated in cases of existing blood dyscrasias, bone marrow depression	✓	✓	✓	✓			
Contraindicated in preexisting liver damage	✓	✓	✓	✓			

TABLE 13 Continued.

	1 - 2 mg						5 - 10 mg	
	U.S.A.	Mexico	Central America	Brazil	Argentina		Mexico	Brazil
CONTRAINDICATIONS AND WARNINGS, Continued								
Caution in patients hypersensitive to any phenothiazine	√							
Warn patients about activities requiring alertness	√							
Caution in pregnant women	√	√	√	√				
Caution in patients with angina, impaired cardiovascular system	√	√	√	√	√			
Warning of blood dyscrasias, hepatitis, liver damage	√	√	√	√				
Warning of retinopathy	√							
May mask signs of overdosage of toxic drugs, obscure diagnosis of intestinal obstruction, brain tumor, etc.	√	√	√	√				
Additive effects with sedatives, narcotics, anesthetics, tranquilizers, alcohol	√	√	√	√				
With prolonged administration at high doses, may be sudden onset of severe central nervous system or vasomotor symptoms	√							
NONE LISTED								X
ADVERSE REACTIONS:								
Drowsiness, somnolence	√	√	√	√	√		√	√
Dizziness	√				√		√	√
Skin reactions	√	√b	√b	√	√			√
Insomnia	√	√	√	√				√
Mouth dryness	√	√	√	√				√
Amenorrhea	√							
Fatigue	√	√	√	√				
Muscular weakness	√							√
Anorexia	√				√		√	
Lactation	√						√	
Blurred vision	√				√		√	√

TABLE 13 Continued.

	1 - 2 mg					5 - 10 mg	
ADVERSE REACTIONS, Continued	U.S.A.	Mexico	Central America	Brazil	Argentina	Mexico	Brazil
Extrapyramidal reactions (motor restlessness, dystonic type or may resemble parkinsonism)	✓						✓
Extrapyramidal symptoms (rarely seen with recommended doses)		✓	✓	✓		✓	
Agitation, jitteriness	✓						
Spasm of neck muscles, torticollis, extensor rigidity of back muscles, opisthotonos, carpopedal spasm, etc.	✓						✓
Pseudoparkinsonism (mask-like facies, drooling, tremors, pill-rolling motion, cogwheel rigidity, etc.)	✓						✓
Persistent tardive dyskinesia (may appear during treatment or after therapy discontinued)	✓						
Hyperreflexia, dystonia, akathisia, dyskinesia, parkinsonism, etc.[c]	✓						
Grand mal convulsions, altered spinal fluid proteins, cerebral edema, prolongation of effects of central nervous system depressants, atropine, heat, organophosphorus insecticides[c]	✓						
Nasal congestion, headache, nausea, constipation, obstipation, adynamic ileus, inhibition of ejaculation[c]	✓						
Reactivation of psychotic processes, catatonic-like states[c]	✓						
Hypotension (sometimes fatal), cardiac arrest[c]	✓						
Hypotension, tachycardia						✓	
Pancytopenia, thrombocytopenic purpura, leukopenia, agranulocytosis, eosinophilia[c]	✓						
Liver damage: jaundice, biliary stasis[c]	✓						

TABLE 13 Continued

	1 - 2 mg					5 - 10 mg	
	U.S.A.	Mexico	Central America	Brazil	Argentina	Mexico	Brazil
ADVERSE REACTIONS, Continued							
Galactorrhea, gynecomastia, menstrual irregularities, false positive pregnancy tests[c]	√						
Photosensitivity, itching, erythema, urticaria, eczema[c]	√						
Allergic reactions (asthma, laryngeal edema, angioneurotic edema, anaphylactoid reactions)[c]	√						
Peripheral edema, reversed epinephrine effect, hyperpyrexia, systemic lupus erythematosus-like syndrome[c]	√						
Pigmentary retinopathy, skin pigmentation, lenticular and corneal deposits, electrocardiogram changes[c]	√						
Asphyxia due to failure of cough reflex (sometimes fatal)[c]	√						
With use of recommended dose, secondary effects have not been frequent, and have been benign and transient		√	√	√			

[a]"Possibly effective."

[b]Mild reactions.

[c]Have occurred with one or more phenothiazine products.

NOTE: Explanation of the sources of information in this table will be found on page ix.

7.

ANTIDEPRESSANTS

Selected for examination in this chapter is the published information presented on a group of widely used antidepressants:

— imipramine (marketed by Geigy as Tofranil)

— desipramine (marketed by Lakeside as Norpramin and Norpolake)

— nortriptyline (marketed by Lilly as Aventyl and Avantyl)

— phenelzine (marketed by Warner-Chilcott as Nardil)

The first three are generally classified as tricyclic substances, the last as a monoamine oxidase (MAO) inhibitor.

Until the late 1950s, the main treatments for mental depression were psychotherapy for mild forms and electroconvulsive shock therapy for more severe cases. Various stimulant drugs had been investigated but with limited success.[1] Then, in 1957, the first of the MAO inhibitors was introduced, followed in 1958 by the first of the tricyclic antidepressants.

Widespread use of these agents during the past fifteen years has clearly demonstrated both their values and their hazards. In general, it appears, most clinicians agree that the tricyclics are essentially alike in their efficacy and their side effects.[2] They are also substantially more effective and safer than the MAO inhibitors.[3] Hollister has stated that the MAO inhibitors should be thought of as last-choice agents, to be used only when other drugs have failed.[4] There is some indication that the tricyclic compounds may be useful in controlling bed-wetting in children and adolescents.[5]

Associated with use of the antidepressants in general and the MAO inhibitors in particular are well-documented hazards. Antidepressants should be used with caution in patients who are agitated or hyperactive, and in those with epilepsy, glaucoma, renal failure, or severely impaired liver function. Special care is required when they are used with other drugs that lower blood pressure.[6] The tricyclic agents are specifically contraindicated in the presence of congestive heart failure and paroxysmal tachycardia and in patients using guanethidine. Caution is needed when these agents are administered to patients also taking barbiturates, adrenergic agents, anticholinergic agents, or thyroid.

The MAO inhibitors are contraindicated in the presence of confirmed or suspected cerebrovascular defect, hypertension, cardiovascular disease, and pheochromocytoma. They are known to potentiate the effects of a considerable number of drugs, including barbiturates, insulin, procaine, adrenergic agents, antiparkinsonism agents, and meperidine.[7]

Particular risk is associated with the use of a tricyclic antidepressant by a patient also taking an MAO inhibitor. The results may be tremors, fever, generalized clonic convulsions, delirium, or death. It is recommended that no tricyclic antidepressant be given without waiting at least two weeks after an MAO inhibitor is discontinued; four days should elapse between termination of tricyclic antidepressant therapy and the start of an MAO inhibitor.[8]

Among the most serious adverse reactions charged to the MAO inhibitors are those involving the liver, the brain, and the cardiovascular system. The toxicity of these drugs as a group has been described as "greater and more serious than that of any other drug used for the treatment of mental illness."[9] They are known to produce serious or even life-threatening hypertensive crises, acute cardiac failure, and intracranial bleeding when patients are also using foods rich in tyramine and other pressor amines, such as aged cheeses, aged wines, pickled herring, and chocolate.[10]

For the tricyclic drugs, it has been noted that all can cause serious adverse effects. Some reaction occurs in about 15 percent of the users and severe reactions in about 5 percent. Among the serious effects are psychosis, hallucinations, hypotension, myocardial infarction, and strokes, especially in patients with cardiovascular disease. Still other adverse reactions, especially in older patients, include urinary retention and paralytic ileus.[11]

LABELING

Imipramine

The description of Tofranil in *PDR* conforms to the view that tricyclic antidepressants are useful drugs whose use involves a high degree of risk. It is presented as effective in the relief of symptoms of depression, and probably useful in the control of some cases of childhood enuresis (Table 14). In the Latin American countries, its use against depression is presented in great detail, along with its value in the treatment of enuresis and nocturnal fears in children and the control of spasmodic or compulsive crying and "emotional incontinence" in geriatric patients. In Mexico, it is listed as indicated broadly in the treatment of "emotional disorders," while Central American physicians are told it is also useful in the treatment of chronic alcoholism and parkinsonism.

Physicians in the United States are advised that use of Tofranil concomitantly with MAO inhibitors is contraindicated, since serious or fatal drug-drug interactions may occur. Caution is urged in its use by pregnant women — since fetal malformations have been reported — and by children and patients with cardiovascular disease, hyperthyroid disease, or increased intraocular pressure, and those in the acute recovery period after myocardial infarction. Few such warnings are presented in Latin America. The dangers of a life-threatening interaction with an MAO inhibitor is noted in Central America and Argentina but not in Mexico, Colombia, Ecuador, or Brazil.

In the same way, while physicians in the United States are informed that adverse reactions to Tofranil may include such serious conditions as myocardial infarction, apoplectic stroke, hypertension, exacerbation of psychosis, seizures, and bone-marrow depression, Latin American physicians are informed mainly of such reactions as mouth dryness, disturbances of accommodation, constipation, itching, and perspiration.

Desipramine

In the United States, Norpramin is said to be useful solely for the relief of symptoms of depression. Its use in children is not recommended. In Latin America, it is described as useful in a variety of depressive states and, in Colombia and Ecuador, for the control of bed-wetting (Table 15).

The concomitant use of the drug with MAO inhibitors is contraindicated in the United States, Mexico, Central America, and Argentina, but not in Colombia or Ecuador. While many serious adverse reactions are listed in the United States, only palpitations, mouth dryness, dizziness, and headache are noted in Mexico. In Central America, Colombia, Ecuador, and Argentina, no adverse reactions are listed.

Nortriptyline

The indications listed for this product, marketed in the United States as Aventyl and in Mexico as Avantyl, are essentially the same and are limited solely to the relief of symptoms of depression (Table 16). In both the United States and Mexico, there appears to be essentially the same description of contraindications and warnings, including a contraindication of concurrent treatment with MAO inhibitors, and a full disclosure of potential adverse reactions.

In Argentina, the indications include such conditions as psychoneurosis, nail-biting and enuresis in children, psychosomatic reactions, alcoholism, senile psychosis, schizophrenia, and mental retardation. Use of the drug with MAO inhibitors and in patients with glaucoma or a history of urinary retention is contraindicated, and caution is urged with the concomitant use of sympathomimetic drugs. No adverse reactions are listed. It should be recalled, however, that the descriptions in the Argentine reference book are prepared by an independent panel of editors and are not the responsibility of the drug manufacturer.

Phenelzine

In the views of at least some authoritative publications, as noted above, MAO inhibitors as a class are less useful than tricyclic compounds in the treatment of depression and significantly more dangerous. This is reflected in the statements presented for Nardil in *PDR*, which indicate the product is only "possibly" effective in the treatment of moderate to severe depressive states in adults. It is not indicated for the control of mild depression or of the depression that represents an appropriate response to the temporary stress (Table 17). In Latin America, it is held to be more widely useful. In Central America, for example, it is described as indicated for all forms of depression and for states of stress and anxiety, and as an adjunct in the treatment of psychosomatic illnesses.

In the United States, Nardil is contraindicated with the concurrent use of other MAO inhibitors or of tricyclic drugs. No such warning is presented in Mexico, Central America, or Argentina. In the same way, in the United States use of the drug is contraindicated in patients receiving such central nervous system depressants as alcohol and narcotics, since fatal reactions have occurred. This warning, too, is not mentioned in Mexico, Central America, or Argentina. In these Latin American countries, few contraindications and warnings are noted. In Central America and in Argentina, no adverse reactions are listed.

TABLE 14. *Information given on:*

IMIPRAMINE
marketed as TOFRANIL (Geigy).

	U.S.A.	Mexico	Central America	Ecuador, Colombia	Brazil	Argentina
INDICATIONS FOR USE:						
Relief of symptoms of depression	√a	√	√	√	√	√
Depressions due to regressive phenomena (the climacteric, involution, presenility and senility		√	√	√		
Depressions caused by arteriosclerosis		√	√	√		
Depressed states with psychopathic basis		√	√	√	√	
Reactive depressions		√	√	√		
Neurotic depressions		√	√	√	√	
Larvate depressions		√		√		
Periodic and simple melancholy, involutional depression		√	√	√		
Symptomatic depression		√				
Involutional, neurotic, psychoreactional, psychoasthenic depression					√	
"Dissipates depression, normalizes state of mind, and modifies emotional disorders"						√
In pediatrics:						
Dysphoric states		√		√		
Disthymias		√		√		
Neurotic or reactive depressions		√	√	√		
Nocturnal fear, terror		√	√	√	√	√
Behavioral disorders					√	√
Childhood enuresis	√b	√	√	√	√	√
Enuresis of adolescence		√				
Psychopathic depression (and somatic equivalents)		√				
In geriatrics:						
Emotional disorders		√				
Spasmodic or compulsive crying		√	√	√		
Emotional incontinence		√	√	√		√
Mood disorders			√			√

TABLE 14 Continued.

	U.S.A.	Mexico	Central America	Ecuador, Colombia	Brazil	Argentina
INDICATIONS FOR USE, Continued						
Obsessive symptoms, depressive disthymias in geriatric disorders						✓
Depressive syndrome due to senility, apoplexy, hypochondria, chronic somatic illness		✓	✓	✓		
Depressive syndrome due to chronic painful states			✓			
Chronic alcoholism, parkinsonism			✓			
CONTRAINDICATIONS AND WARNINGS:						
Contraindicated with use of monoamine oxidase inhibitors	✓c		✓			✓
Hypersensitivity (may be cross-sensitivity with other dibenzazepines	✓	✓		✓		
Contraindicated in acute recovery period after myocardial infarction	✓					
Caution in pregnant women	✓d				✓	
Contraindicated during first trimester of pregnancy		✓				
Caution in lactating mothers	✓					
Caution in patients with cardiovascular disease	✓		✓		✓	
Caution in patients with increased intraocular pressure, history of urinary retention, narrow-angle glaucoma, history of seizures, hyperthyroid disease or receiving thyroid medication, or receiving guanethidine or anticholinergic agents	✓					
Caution in patients with prostatic hypertrophy			✓	✓	✓	✓
Caution in patients with urinary tract disorders			✓			
Caution in elderly patients with urinary tract disorders					✓	
Caution in patients with accentuated tendency for convulsions			✓			
Use in children not recommended	✓e				✓f	
May impair mental and/or physical abilities required to perform hazardous tasks	✓					

TABLE 14 Continued.

	U.S.A.	Mexico	Central America	Ecuador, Colombia	Brazil	Argentina
CONTRAINDICATIONS AND WARNINGS, Continued						
Hypomanic or manic disorders may occur	✓					
Discontinue drug prior to elective surgery	✓					
May activate psychosis in schizophrenics	✓					
May exaggerate response to alcohol	✓					✓
Caution with patients on electroshock therapy	✓					
May elevate or lower blood-sugar levels	✓					
Caution in patients "who show a certain neuro-vegetative lability"					✓	
May be increase in spasmophilia					✓	
Caution in patients with disorders of stimulus conduction			✓			
Do blood study if fever or sore throat develops	✓					
ADVERSE REACTIONS:						
Hypertension, hypotension, palpitation, myocardial infarction, arrhythmias, heart block, stroke, falls	✓					
Confusional states with hallucinations, disorientation, delusions, anxiety, restlessness, agitation, insomnia, nightmares, hypomania, exacerbation of psychosis	✓					
Numbness, tingling, paresthesias of the extremities, incoordination, ataxia, tremors, peripheral neuropathy, extrapyramidal symptoms, seizures, alteration in EEG patterns, tinnitus	✓					
Mouth dryness	✓	✓		✓		
Blurred vision, etc.	✓					
Disturbances of accommodation	✓	✓		✓		
Constipation	✓	✓		✓		
Paralytic ileus	✓					
Urinary retention, delayed micturition, dilation of urinary tract, urinary frequency	✓					

TABLE 14 Continued.

	U.S.A.	Mexico	Central America	Ecuador,Colombia	Brazil	Argentina
ADVERSE REACTIONS, Continued						
Skin rash, petechiae, urticaria, photosensitization, edema, drug fever, cross-sensitivity with other tricyclic drugs	√					
Itching	√	√		√		
Bone marrow depression	√					
Nausea, vomiting, anorexia, epigastric distress, diarrhea, stomatitis, abdominal cramps, etc.	√					
Perspiration	√	√		√		
Gynecomastia, breast enlargement and galactorrhea, increased or decreased libido, impotence, etc.	√					
Elevation or depression of blood-sugar levels	√					
Jaundice, altered liver function, weight gain or loss, flushing, drowsiness, weakness, fatigue, headache, parotid swelling, alopecia	√					
NONE LISTED			X		X	X

[a]Endogenous depressions more likely to be alleviated than others.

[b]May be useful as temporary adjunctive therapy in reducing enuresis in children 6 years and older after possible organic causes ruled out.

[c]Fatalities have occurred.

[d]Congenital malformations have been reported.

[e]Administration of drug in pediatric conditions other than enuresis or in children younger than 6 years not recommended; safety in long-term, chronic use in children not established.

[f]Caution in "young individuals."

NOTE: Explanation of the sources of information in this table will be found on page ix.

TABLE 15. *Information given on:*

DESIPRAMINE

marketed as NORPRAMIN, NORPOLAKE (Lakeside).

	U.S.A.	Mexico	Central America	Ecuador, Colombia	Argentina
INDICATIONS FOR USE:					
Relief of symptoms of depression	√a	√	√	√	√
Manic-depressive, psychotic-depressive, psycho-neurotic depressive reactions		√	√	√	
For elderly patients with depressive syndromes caused by senility and chronic illness		√			
For patients with symptoms such as sadness, crying spells, insomnia, hopelessness, emptiness, personal devaluation, fatigue, tachycardia, constipation, loss of libido, etc.		√	√		
Involutional psychotic reactions of depressive type				√	
Nocturnal enuresis				√	
Psychotic, psychoneurotic, and postpartum depressions					√
Anxiety secondary to depression					√
Gastrointestinal, dermatological, and other disorders associated with depression					√
Depressive disorders induced by menopause and andropause					√
CONTRAINDICATIONS AND WARNINGS:					
Contraindicated with use of monoamine oxidase inhibitors	√b	√	√		√
Contraindicated in hypersensitivity (may be cross-sensitivity with other dibenzazepines)	√				
Contraindicated in acute recovery period after myocardial infarction	√	√	√		
Caution in patients with cardiovascular disease	√	√c	√c	√c	√c
Caution in patients with history of urinary retention	√				
Caution in patients with glaucoma	√	√d	√d	√d	√d
Caution in patients with thyroid disease or taking thyroid medication	√				√

TABLE 15 Continued.

	U.S.A.	Mexico	Central America	Ecuador, Colombia	Argentina
CONTRAINDICATIONS AND WARNINGS, Continued					
Caution in patients with history of seizures	✓	✓d	✓d		✓
Caution in patients receiving guanethidine or similarly acting drugs, anticholinergic or sympathomimetic drugs	✓				
Not recommended for use in children	✓				
Caution patient about performing hazardous tasks or operating machinery	✓				
Dispense in least possible quantities, since suicide associated with this class of drugs	✓				
Caution in pregnant women, nursing mothers	✓		✓		
May induce hypomanic state	✓				
May cause exacerbation of psychosis in schizophrenia	✓				
Discontinue drug prior to elective surgery	✓				
Do blood study if fever or sore throat develops during therapy	✓				
May elevate or lower blood-sugar levels	✓				
Contraindicated in patients with urethral or ureteral spasm		✓	✓		✓
May exaggerate response to alcohol	✓				
ADVERSE REACTIONS:					
Hypotension, hypertension, tachycardia, arrhythmias, heart block, myocardial infarction, stroke	✓				
Palpitations	✓	✓			
Confusional states with hallucinations, disorientation, delusions, anxiety, restlessness, agitation, insomnia, nightmares, hypomania, exacerbation of psychosis	✓				
Numbness, tingling, paresthesias of the extremities, incoordination, ataxia, tremors, peripheral neuropathy, extrapyramidal symptoms, seizures, alteration in EEG patterns, tinnitus	✓				
Mouth dryness	✓	✓			

TABLE 15 Continued.

	U.S.A.	Mexico	Central America	Ecuador, Colombia	Argentina
ADVERSE REACTIONS, Continued					
Blurred vision, disturbances of accommodation, mydriasis	✓				
Constipation, paralytic ileus	✓				
Urinary retention, delayed micturition, dilation of urinary tract, urinary frequency	✓				
Skin rash, petechiae, urticaria, itching, photo-sensitization, edema, drug fever, cross-sensitivity with other tricyclic drugs	✓				
Bone marrow depression	✓				
Nausea, vomiting, anorexia, epigastric distress, diarrhea, stomatitis, abdominal cramps, etc.	✓				
Gynecomastia, breast enlargement and galactorrhea, increased or decreased libido, impotence, etc.	✓				
Elevation or depression of blood-sugar levels	✓				
Jaundice, altered liver function, weight gain or loss, flushing, drowsiness, weakness, fatigue, parotid swelling, alopecia, perspiration	✓				
Dizziness, headache	✓	✓			
NONE LISTED			X	X	X

[a]Endogenous depressions more likely to be alleviated than others.

[b]Fatalities have occurred.

[c]Contraindicated in severe coronary disease with electrocardiographic abnormalities.

[d]Contraindicated.

NOTE: Explanation of the sources of information in this table will be found on page ix.

TABLE 16. *Information given on:*

NORTRIPTYLINE

marketed as AVENTYL, AVANTYL (Lilly).

	U.S.A.	Mexico	Argentina
INDICATIONS FOR USE:			
Relief of symptoms of depression	✓a	✓a	✓
Treatment of mental depression, nervous tension and anxiety, psychosomatic conditions, adjuvant to psychotherapy			✓
Involutional depression, manic depression, psychotic and reactive depression			✓
Psychoneurosis, anxiety reaction, phobias, or obsessive-compulsive states			✓
Symptomatic reactions in children (nail-biting, enuresis, etc.)			✓
Psychosomatic gastrointestinal reactions, alcoholism, senile psychosis, schizophrenia, mental retardation			✓
CONTRAINDICATIONS AND WARNINGS:			
Contraindicated with use of monoamine oxidase inhibitors	✓b	✓b	✓
Hypersensitivity (may be cross-sensitivity with other dibenzazepines)	✓	✓	
Contraindicated in acute recovery period after myocardial infarction	✓	✓	
Caution in patients with cardiovascular disease	✓	✓	
May block antihypertensive action of guanethidine, etc.	✓	✓	
Caution in patients with glaucoma or history of urinary retention	✓	✓	✓
Caution in patients with history of seizures	✓	✓	
Caution in patients with hyperthyroid disease	✓	✓	
Warn patient to use caution in performing hazardous tasks and operating machinery	✓	✓	
Caution in pregnant women, lactating mothers	✓	✓	
Use in children not recommended	✓		
May activate or exacerbate schizophrenic symptoms	✓	✓	
May increase anxiety and agitation in overactive or agitated patients	✓	✓	
May arouse troublesome patient hostility	✓	✓	
May cause epileptiform seizures	✓	✓	
May exaggerate response to alcohol	✓	✓	

TABLE 16 Continued.

	U.S.A.	Mexico	Argentina
CONTRAINDICATIONS AND WARNINGS, Continued			
Discontinue drug several days prior to elective surgery	✓	✓	
May unchain manic phase in manic-depressive patients		✓	
Caution with concomitant use of other anticholinergic drugs		✓	
Caution with patients on electroconvulsive therapy		✓	
May elevate or decrease blood-sugar level		✓	
Caution with concomitant use of sympathomimetics			✓
ADVERSE REACTIONS:			
Hypotension, hypertension, arrhythmias, heart block, myocardial infarction, stroke, etc.	✓	✓	
Confusional states, hallucinations, disorientation, delusions, anxiety, insomnia, exacerbation of psychosis, etc.	✓	✓	
Restlessness, agitation, panic, nightmares, hypomania	✓		
Peripheral neuropathy, ataxia, convulsions, tinnitus	✓	✓	
Tingling, numbness, paresthesias of extremities, incoordination, tremors, extrapyramidal reactions, seizures, etc.	✓		
Mouth dryness, disturbances of accommodation, constipation, urinary retention	✓	✓	
Blurred vision, mydriasis	✓		
Paralytic ileus	✓		
Allergic cutaneous reactions, photosensitivity, edema, fever, etc.	✓	✓	
Cross-sensitivity to other tricyclic drugs	✓		
Bone marrow depression	✓	✓	
Nausea, vomiting, diarrhea, dyspepsia	✓	✓	
Anorexia, stomatitis, abdominal cramps, etc.	✓		
Gynecomastia, breast enlargement and galactorrhea, changes in libido, impotence	✓	✓	
Jaundice, dizziness, headache, alopecia	✓	✓	
Altered liver function, weight gain or loss, elevation or depression of blood-sugar levels, perspiration, flushing, urinary frequency, nocturia, drowsiness, weakness, fatigue, parotid swelling	✓		
NONE LISTED			X

aEndogenous depressions more likely to be alleviated than others.

bFatalities have occurred.

NOTE: Explanation of the sources of information in this table will be found on page ix.

TABLE 17. *Information given on:*

PHENELZINE

marketed as NARDIL (Warner-Chilcott).

	U.S.A.	Mexico	Central America	Argentina
INDICATIONS FOR USE:				
Endogenous depression	√a	√		√
Depressive phase of manic-depressive psychosis	√a			
Exogenous (reactive) depression	√a	√		√
Senile or involutive depression		√		√
Use in conjunction with tranquilizers for treatment of tension in states of anguish and anxiety		√		
Depressive states in general		√	√	
For states of stress and anxiety		√		
As adjunct in treatment of psychosomatic illnesses (bronchial asthma, mucosal colitis, etc.), making patient more accessible to psychotherapy		√		
Postpartum and postdrug depressions				√
Depression symptomatic of chronic disease				√
Calms anginal pain		√		
CONTRAINDICATIONS AND WARNINGS:				
Contraindicated with use of other monoamine oxidase inhibitors or of dibenzazepine derivatives	√			
Contraindicated in patients with known hypersensitivity to the drug, pheochromocytoma, congestive heart disease, history of liver disease, or abnormal liver function tests	√			
Contraindicated in patients with severe hepatitis			√	√
Contraindicated in patients receiving sympathomimetic drugs, cocaine, or local anesthetics containing sympathomimetic vasoconstrictors, guanethidine	√			
Contraindicated in patients ingesting foods or beverages high in tryptamine or tyramine (e.g., pods of broad beans, aged cheeses, beer, wines, pickled herring, chicken liver, yeast extract)	√			

TABLE 17 Continued.

	U.S.A.	Mexico	Central America	Argentina
CONTRAINDICATIONS AND WARNINGS, Continued				
Contraindicated in patients ingesting aged alcoholic beverages or cheeses		✓		
Contraindicated in patients ingesting excessive amounts of caffeine or chocolate	✓			
Contraindicated in patients receiving such central nervous system depressants as alcohol and narcotics	✓b			
Contraindicated in patients undergoing elective surgery requiring general anesthetics	✓			
Discontinue drug prior to elective surgery	✓			
Not advisable to use in elderly or debilitated patients, or patients with hypertension or cardiovascular or cerebrovascular disease	✓			
Not recommended in patients with frequent or severe headache; discontinue immediately if these occur	✓			
Caution in patients receiving antihypertensive drugs, including thiazide diuretics	✓			
Observe blood pressure frequently to detect evidence of any pressor response	✓			
Warn patients against taking high-tyramine content foods, alcoholic beverages, self-medication with cold and hayfever or reducing preparations	✓			
Caution in pregnant women, lactating mothers	✓			
Not recommended for patients under 16 years of age	✓			
Follow patients closely for symptoms of postural hypotension	✓			
Caution in patients with epilepsy	✓			
Caution in patients receiving Rauwolfia alkaloids	✓			
May cause excessive stimulation in schizophrenics	✓			
Caution in maniacal, agitated, or over-stimulated patients				✓
ADVERSE REACTIONS:				
Dizziness, constipation, mouth dryness, postural hypotension, weakness, fatigue, edema, gastrointestinal disturbances, blurred vision, sweating, urinary				

TABLE 17 Continued.

	U.S.A.	Mexico	Central America	Argentina
ADVERSE REACTIONS, Continued				
retention, euphoria, nystagmus, sexual disturbances, hypernatremia	√	√		
Drowsiness, tremors, twitching, hyperpyrexia, glaucoma, skin rash, jitteriness, palilalia	√			
Ataxia, shock-like coma, edema of glottis, transient respiratory and cardiovascular depression following electroconvulsive therapy, toxic delirium, reversible jaundice, leukopenia, manic reaction, convulsions, acute anxiety reaction, precipitation of schizophrenia	√			
Few cases of fatal progressive necrotizing hepatocellular damage reported	√			
NONE LISTED			X	X

a"Possibly effective" in treatment of moderate to severe depressive states in adults; not indicated in treatment of mild depression or depression that is appropriate response to temporary stress.

bFatalities have occurred.

NOTE: Explanation of the sources of information in this table will be found on page ix.

8.

ANTICONVULSANTS

In this section, three widely used anticonvulsants are examined. These are:

— diphenylhydantoin (marketed by Parke-Davis as Dilantin and Epamin, and by McKesson as Kessodanten and Difenil Hidantoinato MK)

— mephenytoin (marketed by Sandoz as Mesantoin and Mesantoina)

— carbamazepine (marketed by Geigy as Tegretol)

CLINICAL BACKGROUND

In the entire history of medicine, probably no disorder has been "cured" by more numerous and more exotic remedies than epilepsy. Among these ancient curative products were powdered human skull, the fresh blood of a dying Christian gladiator, elk's claw, wolf's liver, the gall of a boar fried in urine, the stones of swallows, opium, hashish, belladonna, turpentine, acids, caustic alkalies, digitalis, and mistletoe — each of them tried, widely accepted, widely used, and eventually rejected as utterly without worth.[1] Until 1938 only two demonstrably useful anticonvulsants had been discovered, the bromides in 1857 and phenobarbital in 1911. Then, in 1938, diphenylhydantoin was introduced into medicine, the first of a whole new class of effective drugs for use in the control of epileptic disorders.

Diphenylhydantoin

Producing antiepileptic effects without causing a general depression of the central nervous system, diphenylhydantoin is widely considered to be the most useful drug for major motor, psychomotor, and other focal types of epilepsy. In some instances, it is used successfully in combination with phenobarbital or primidone. It is, however, regarded as ineffective in petit mal and most minor seizures. Although it has been advocated for use in numerous disorders other than epilepsy, most of these recommendations cannot be substantiated by adequate evidence.[2,3]

The most common toxic effects of the drug involve the central nervous system, the skin, and the mucous membranes. These may include ataxia, hyperactive tendon reflexes, blurring of vision, behavioral changes, and skin and mucous membrane changes that are generally mild but may lead to blindness or death. Hyperplasia of the gums occurs in about 20 percent of all patients undergoing long-term treatment.[4,5]

Life-threatening blood changes, toxic hepatitis, and periarteritis nodosa have been associated with use of the drug. *Medical Letter* consultants state, "Although the side-effects of diphenylhydantoin are usually mild, they are occasionally severe and, rarely, fatal."[6]

Mephenytoin

Soon after its introduction in 1945, mephenytoin, administered together with phenobarbital, was proved to be useful in the treatment of grand mal and other convulsive disorders. Later it was demonstrated to be itself an effective anticonvulsant.[7] Closely related chemically and pharmacologically to diphenylhydantoin, it may sometimes demonstrate dramatic superiority, but this advantage is offset by its greater toxicity.[8] Lupus erythematosus and hepatic damage have been reported, and fatal aplastic anemia and other adverse reactions have occurred.[9] Serious drug-drug interactions have been described.[10]

Carbamazepine

A tricyclic compound related to imipramine, carbamazepine was originally introduced in the United States for the treatment of trigeminal neuralgia and similar disorders. It is described as effective in the relief of pain in both trigeminal and glossopharyngeal neuralgia, multiple sclerosis, acute idiopathic polyneuritis, peripheral diabetic neuropathy, tabes dorsalis, and other disorders. It has also been used to prevent migraine attacks.[11] The major dispute concerning carbamazepine centered around its value in the treatment of epilepsy. Such a use had been accepted for many years in Europe and, as will be noted below, in Latin America, but it was approved by the Food and Drug Administration only in 1974.

Because of the drug's structure, the toxic effects of carbamazepine are similar to those appearing with tricyclic antidepressants. These include such neurologic reactions, occurring in about 15 percent of patients, as dizziness, ataxia, confusion, blurred vision, abnormal involuntary movements, peripheral neuritis, and depression with agitation. Disorders of the digestive tract, including nausea, gastric distress, and abdominal pain, occur in about 4 percent. There may be serious or life-threatening skin reactions in about 2 percent. There may also be transitory or serious blood changes, aggravation of hypertension, hypotension, congestive heart failure, recurrence of thrombophlebitis, and acute urinary retention.[12,13] In general, it should be used cautiously in patients with cardiovascular, liver, renal, or urinary tract disease, or increased intraocular pressure, and in those receiving monoamine oxidase inhibitors or tricyclic antidepressants.[14] Its safety in pregnancy has not been established.

LABELING

Diphenylhydantoin

In the United States, Mexico, Central America, Colombia, Ecuador, and Argentina, Parke-Davis' Dilantin or Epamin is described as indicated for the control of grand mal and psychomotor epilepsy (Table 18). In Colombia and Ecuador, it is listed as useful also in the control of certain cardiac arrhythmias and tachycardia. Numerous contraindications and warnings are presented to physicians in the United States, but few are noted in Mexico and none is listed in Central America, Colombia, Ecuador, or Argentina. In the United States, the listed adverse reactions include such central nervous system

effects as ataxia and confusion, serious or fatal dermatological manifestations, serious or fatal blood dyscrasias, and serious or fatal toxic
hepatitis and periarteritis nodosa. In Mexico, Colombia, and Ecuador,
only relatively mild adverse reactions are included. No adverse
reactions are described in Central America or Argentina.

McKesson's Kessodanten or Difenil Hidantoinato MK is described in
the United States, Central America, Colombia, and Ecuador as
indicated for the control of grand mal and psychomotor epilepsy, and
in the United States for use in selected vascular headaches and
trigeminal neuralgia. Many contraindications and warnings are presented in the United States, and emphasis is placed on serious and
potentially fatal adverse reactions. In Central America, Colombia,
and Ecuador, no adverse reactions are mentioned.

Mephenytoin

Mesantoin is described in the United States as indicated for the control
of grand mal, focal, Jacksonian, and psychomotor seizures that are
refractory to other drugs (Table 19). Generally similar indications are
listed in Mexico, Central America, Colombia, and Ecuador. Physicians in the latter two countries are told that the product is indicated
especially in the treatment of children.

In all the countries concerned here, physicians are warned to
conduct blood examinations periodically. Numerous other warnings
and contraindications are presented in the United States, Colombia,
and Ecuador, and a few in Mexico, but no others in Central America.

Physicians in the United States are informed that potential adverse
reactions include various blood dyscrasias, effects on the central
nervous system, hepatitis, jaundice, and nephrosis. It is emphasized
that some of these reactions may be fatal. Relatively few adverse effects
are listed in Mexico, and the possibility of death is not mentioned.
None is listed in Central America, Colombia, or Ecuador.

Carbamazepine

In the United States and the Latin American countries, Tegretol is
described as useful in the control of certain types of epilepsy (Table

20). In the United States, however, its use is recommended only in patients who have not responded satisfactorily to treatment with other agents. It is also listed as useful in the treatment of trigeminal neuralgia and glossopharyngeal neuralgia. In Brazil and Argentina, indications include the treatment of behavioral disorders in infancy and adolescence.

In *PDR*, special type is used to warn physicians that deaths from aplastic anemia have been reported following treatment with Tegretol and that other serious blood dyscrasias have been observed. A special note states that "since this drug is not a simple analgesic, it should not be used for the relief of trivial aches or pains." No such warning is included in the Latin American descriptions. Physicians in all the countries except Argentina are urged to conduct blood studies regularly during the course of treatment. Relatively few other warnings are listed in the Latin American countries and none in Argentina.

In the same way, *PDR* includes an extensive list of potential adverse reactions, some of them serious or fatal, affecting a variety of body systems. Few of these are mentioned in Mexico, Colombia, and Ecuador, and the possibility of a fatal reaction is not mentioned. No adverse reactions are listed in Central America, Brazil, and Argentina.

TABLE 18. *Information given on:*

DIPHENYLHYDANTOIN

marketed as DILANTIN, EPAMIN (Parke-Davis), KESSODANTEN, DIFENIL HIDANTOINATO MK (McKesson).

	Parke-Davis					McKesson		
	U.S.A.	Mexico	Central America	Ecuador, Colombia	Argentina	U.S.A.	Central America	Ecuador, Colombia
INDICATIONS FOR USE:								
Control of grand mal and psycho-motor seizures	✓	✓	✓	✓	✓	✓	✓a	✓
Control of Jacksonian epilepsy							✓a	✓
Symptomatic relief of selected vascular headaches (migraine), trigeminal neuralgia						✓		
Control of cardiac arrhythmias and paroxysmal tachycardia produced by digitalis, cardiac disease, surgery				✓				
CONTRAINDICATIONS AND WARNINGS:								
Contraindicated in patients with sensitivity to hydantoin products	✓	✓				✓		
Abrupt withdrawal in epileptic patients may precipitate status epilepticus	✓					✓		
Caution in concomitant use of barbiturates, coumarin anticoagulants, disulfiram, phenylbutazone, isoniazid, tricyclic antidepressants	✓					✓		
Caution in concomitant use of phenyramidol, sulfaphenazole						✓		
May interfere with laboratory tests	✓							
Caution in pregnancy, impaired liver function, elderly or gravely ill patients	✓					✓		
Caution in young patients, obese patients						✓		
Discontinue drug if skin rash appears	✓					✓		

TABLE 18 Continued.

	Parke-Davis					McKesson		
	U.S.A.	Mexico	Central America	Ecuador, Colombia	Argentina	U.S.A.	Central America	Ecuador, Colombia
CONTRAINDICATIONS AND WARNINGS, Continued								
Regular hematologic examinations recommended						✓		
May exacerbate petit mal seizures						✓		
Alcohol may interfere with drug action						✓		
Contraindicated in patients with severe coronary disease		✓						
Substitution of one drug for another in epileptic treatment should be done gradually to avoid recurrence of attacks							✓	✓
NONE LISTED			X	X	X			
ADVERSE REACTIONS:								
Gingival hyperplasia	✓	✓		✓		✓		
Nystagmus	✓	✓		✓		✓		
Ataxia	✓	✓						
Diplopia		✓						
Slurred speech, mental confusion, headache	✓					✓		
Dizziness, insomnia, transient nervousness, motor twitchings	✓							
Behavioral changes (hyperactivity, hallucinations, dullness, drowsiness)						✓		
Convulsive manifestations						✓		
Neuropathy, areflexia						✓		
Anorexia						✓		
Nausea, vomiting	✓					✓		
Constipation	✓							
Gastric distress, acute gastric upsets						✓		
Hematemesis						✓b		

TABLE 18 Continued.

	Parke-Davis					McKesson		
	U.S.A.	Mexico	Central America	Ecuador, Colombia	Argentina	U.S.A.	Central America	Ecuador, Colombia
ADVERSE REACTIONS, Continued								
Cutaneous reactions (rashes, exfoliative dermatitis, lupus erythematosus, Stevens-Johnson syndrome, etc.)	✓b					✓b		
Blood dyscrasias	✓b					✓		
Toxic hepatitis, liver damage, periarteritis nodosa	✓b							
Hepatitis, jaundice						✓		
Polyarthropathy	✓							
Hirsutism	✓					✓		
Urinary incontinence						✓		
Dyspnea						✓		
Isolated cases of allergic phenomena				✓				
NONE LISTED			X		X		X	X

aIn combination with phenobarbital.

bMay be fatal.

NOTE: Explanation of the sources of information in this table will be found on page ix.

TABLE 19. *Information given on:*
MEPHENYTOIN
marketed as MESANTOIN, MESANTOINA (Sandoz).

	U.S.A.	Mexico	Central America	Ecuador, Colombia
INDICATIONS FOR USE:				
Control of grand mal, Jacksonian, psychomotor seizures	✓a	✓	✓	✓
Control of focal seizures	✓a	✓	✓	
In electroshock: to prevent fractures		✓	✓	
For diverse psychomotor manifestations, especially in children				✓
CONTRAINDICATIONS AND WARNINGS:				
Contraindicated in patients hypersensitive to drug	✓	✓		✓
Reduce dose gradually to minimize risk of precipitating seizures	✓			
Caution in pregnancy	✓			
Liver screening tests should precede introduction of drug	✓			
Blood examinations recommended during initial phase of administration	✓	✓	✓	✓
Alert patient to signs of blood dyscrasias	✓			
Contraindicated in patients with hypotension, anemia		✓		✓
Discontinue treatment if leukopenia develops	✓			✓
Discontinue treatment if scarlatiniform rash develops				✓
ADVERSE REACTIONS:				
Leukopenia, neutropenia, agranulocytosis, aplastic anemia, other blood dyscrasias	✓			
Blood dyscrasias		✓		
Skin and mucous membrane manifestations (some fatal)	✓			
Dysarthria, fatigue, ataxia, irritability, choreiform movements, depression, tremor, nervousness, sleeplessness, dizziness, mental confusion, psychotic disturbances, increased seizures	✓			
Diplopia, nystagmus, drowsiness, somnolence	✓	✓		
Nausea, vomiting, gum hyperplasia	✓	✓		

TABLE 19 Continued.

	U.S.A.	Mexico	Central America	Ecuador, Colombia
ADVERSE REACTIONS, Continued				
Hepatitis, jaundice, nephrosis, weight gain, edema, etc.	√			
Headache		√		
NONE LISTED			X	X

aIndicated if condition refractory to other drugs.

NOTE: Explanation of the sources of information in this table will be found on page ix.

TABLE 20. *Information given on:*

CARBAMAZEPINE

marketed as TEGRETOL (CIBA-Geigy).

	U.S.A.	Mexico	Central America	Ecuador, Colombia	Brazil	Argentina
INDICATIONS FOR USE:						
Partial seizures with complex symptomatology (psychomotor, temporal)	√a	√	√	√	√	√
Generalized tonic-clonic seizures (grand mal)	√a	√	√	√	√	√
Mixed seizure patterns	√a	√	√	√	√	√
Epilepsy with predominant psychic manifestations (including petit mal attacks)		√b		√b		
Focal crisis		√	√	√		√
Petit mal					√b	
Epilepsy with exclusively psychic symptoms			√			
Epileptic alterations in personality						√
Treatment of pain associated with trigeminal neuralgia	√	√	√	√	√	√
Trigeminal neuralgia in multiple sclerosis		√	√	√		
Other facial neuralgias					√	
Diverse neurologic algias				√		
Central diabetes insipidus			√			
Polydipsia, polyuria of neurohormonal origin			√			
Infantile and adolescent behavioral disorders					√	√
Glossopharyngeal neuralgia	√	√	√	√		√
CONTRAINDICATIONS AND WARNINGS:						
Contraindicated in patients with history of previous bone marrow depression	√					
Contraindicated in patients with hypersensitivity to the drug	√					
Contraindicated in patients with hypersensitivity to any tricyclic compound	√	√		√		
Use with monoamine oxidase inhibitors not recommended	√	√				

TABLE 20 Continued.

	U.S.A.	Mexico	Central America	Ecuador, Colombia	Brazil	Argentina
CONTRAINDICATIONS AND WARNINGS, Continued						
Discontinue use if evidence of significant bone marrow depression occurs	✓					
Contraindicated for relief of trivial aches or pains	✓					
Caution in women of childbearing potential	✓					
Caution in elderly patients	✓					
Inadvisable for mothers using drug to nurse infants	✓					
Caution in patients with increased intraocular pressure	✓					
Consider possibility of activating latent psychosis	✓					
Pretreatment blood examinations should be performed	✓					
Regular blood examinations should be performed during treatment	✓	✓	✓	✓	✓	
Baseline and periodic evaluation of liver function should be obtained	✓					
Baseline and periodic eye examinations, urinalysis, etc., recommended	✓					
Reduction in dose should be gradual		✓	✓	✓		
Patient should be watched for appearance of allergic cutaneous manifestations					✓	
Caution patient about hazards of operating machinery or automobiles	✓					
Treatment should always be carried out under medical supervision					✓	
NONE LISTED						X
ADVERSE REACTIONS:						
Dizziness, vertigo	✓	✓		✓		
Drowsiness, somnolence	✓	✓		✓		
Unsteadiness	✓					
Nausea, vomiting	✓	✓		✓		
Aplastic anemia, leukopenia, agranulocytosis, etc.	✓					
Abnormalities in liver function, jaundice	✓					

TABLE 20 Continued.

	U.S.A.	Mexico	Central America	Ecuador, Colombia	Brazil	Argentina
ADVERSE REACTIONS, Continued						
Urinary frequency, acute urinary retention, oliguria with elevated blood pressure, impotence	✓					
Disturbances of coordination, confusion, headache, fatigue, blurred vision, visual hallucinations, peripheral neuritis, etc.	✓					
Asthenia, hypotonia, laxity, fainting		✓		✓		
Depression with agitation, hallucinations, nystagmus, tinnitus, hyperacusis	✓					
Pruritic and erythematous rashes, urticaria, Stevens-Johnson syndrome, photosensitivity, exfoliative dermatitis, etc.	✓					
Allergic dermatosis		✓		✓		
Gastric distress, constipation, mouth dryness	✓					
Anorexia	✓	✓		✓		
Congestive heart failure, aggravation of hypertension, hypotension, syncope and collapse, edema, thrombophlebitis, aggravation of coronary artery disease, etc.	✓c					
Cortical lens opacities, conjunctivitis	✓					
Aching joints and muscles, leg cramps	✓					
Fever, chills	✓					
NONE LISTED			X		X	X

aFor patients who have not responded satisfactorily to other agents; not recommended as drug of choice.

bIn association with specific anticonvulsants.

cFatalities reported.

NOTE: Explanation of the sources of information in this table will be found on page ix.

9.

DISCUSSION: THE EPIDEMIOLOGY OF DRUG PROMOTION

It is abundantly clear that there are glaring differences in the ways in which the same multinational pharmaceutical companies describe essentially the same drug products to physicians in the United States and to their medical colleagues in Latin America. This holds not only for global corporations headquartered in the United States. It is true also for such companies based in Switzerland, France, West Germany, and other nations.

In the United States, the indications or approved uses published in *Physicians' Desk Reference* are generally brief, specific, and concise, and limited to those that can be supported by substantial scientific evidence accepted by the Food and Drug Administration. The contra-indications, warnings, and adverse reactions are presented in great detail. This full disclosure of unpleasant, dangerous, or potentially lethal side effects is required by United States laws, laws that are vigorously enforced by FDA. In addition, and perhaps coincidentally, drug company attorneys have looked upon full disclosure of possible hazards not only as clinically essential and socially desirable but also as one important ingredient in their efforts to protect their firms against lawsuits involving product liability.

For whatever reasons, the reverse situation is evident in Latin America. With few exceptions, the indications included in the reference books are far more extensive, but the listings of hazards are curtailed, glossed over, or totally omitted. In some cases, only trivial side effects are described, while serious or possibly fatal reactions are not mentioned.

It is important to stress that the differences are not simply between the United States on the one hand and all the Latin American countries on the other. There are substantial differences *within* Latin America. The same multinational company marketing the same drug may describe it in one way in Mexico, tell a different story in Guatemala, Nicaragua, El Salvador, Honduras, Costa Rica, Panama, and the Dominican Republic, use still a different approach in Colombia and Ecuador, and yet another in Brazil. It may list certain indications for the product in one country but different indications in another. It may make reasonably full disclosure of serious side effects in one nation but ignore some or all of them in another. In some instances, the identical drug marketed by two competing companies is described differently in the identical country. If there are corporate or national patterns or policies to explain these variations, they are not readily discernible.

These and other discrepancies are evident for virtually all the products surveyed in this study and for many others not reviewed here. It must be emphasized, however, that Latin America has not been singled out for such treatment by multinational companies. Similar differences in the case of chloramphenicol are apparent also in such non-third-world nations as France, Italy, Spain, Australia, and New Zealand.[1]

The problem has been further complicated by another factor. In the United States, Canada, the United Kingdom, and most European countries, all the drugs discussed here are so-called prescription drugs, available only with a physician's prescription. In most of Latin America, a physician's prescription may be legally required, but we have observed that many patients commonly and openly obtain the products directly from a pharmacist—or an untrained pharmacist's assistant—without a prescription of any kind. This practice may be against the law, but it is usually said that "the government looks the other way." Sometimes the patient may ask for a specific drug by name, often on the recommendation of a neighbor, friend, or relative. Or the patient will describe his symptoms and the pharmacist will then diagnose, prescribe, and dispense. If the drug must be given by injection, many a pharmacist will oblige. This, too, is banned by law, but here again "the government looks the other way." If a pharmacist is found to be breaking such laws, he is usually given a mild reprimand or required to pay a minuscule fine. If the patient is injured by this variety of therapy, it is rare for the pharmacist to be punished.

Of Company Attitudes

The policies and decisions of the Food and Drug Administration, as reflected in the drug descriptions approved for publication in *Physicians' Desk Reference*, have been criticized on many grounds by both physicians and industry representatives. It has been charged that FDA has refused to accept indications for some applications, even though what some physicians consider adequate supportive evidence is available. The potential hazards are described in such complete detail that many physicians have neither the time nor the patience to read them, and accordingly such full disclosure may be self-defeating. Full disclosure of hazards, the critics say, is unnecessary because "physicians are already aware of them." The listing of dangers is said to be so extensive, including both proved and merely suspected hazards, that many physicians may become needlessly alarmed; as a result, their patients may not get a drug that could benefit them. On the other hand, physicians may choose to ignore the warnings, just as many U.S. physicians — like their patients — have chosen to ignore the warnings carried in all cigarette promotion.

Perhaps most important, it is claimed that some disputes between FDA on the one hand and industry spokesmen on the other represent "honest differences of opinion" on complex points where not all experts agree. In some instances, there may be conflicting evidence, and FDA has made what have been termed capricious, arbitrary, or erroneous decisions.

"There have been plenty of historical examples in which the company has been proven right in its claims and the independent experts who have opposed them have been proven wrong," one authority has stated, "just as there are examples of the reverse."[2]

FDA representatives do not deny such a charge. "But this doesn't happen very often," one said, "and when it does, we back down. We change our decision."

Though some critics have asserted that FDA places excessive emphasis on the potential hazards of a drug, spokesmen for some consumer groups insist the agency has failed to put enough stress on these risks.

Finally, the entire system of drug-labeling regulations in the United States has been denounced as one more instance of unwarranted government interference in the practice of medicine, an unjustified attempt to dictate to a physician how he should prescribe, and a threat to physician-patient relationships. But, as emphasized at the outset, the full-disclosure regulations are intended to enable the physician to make his prescribing judgments with maximum knowledge of the safety and efficacy of each product.

Somewhat similar statements have been made to explain or defend the extraordinary differences in drug labeling and promotion between the United States and Latin America, and particularly the glossing-over of or failure to mention serious or potentially fatal side effects.

In Latin America, as in the United States, it is said by drug companies that full disclosure is unnecessary because all physicians are fully aware of the hazards and need no further warnings. This defense has been bitterly assailed by Latin American medical experts and medical educators and denounced by one distinguished hematologist at Mexico City's National Institute of Cardiology as "not merely nonsense but damnably dangerous nonsense."

The "doctors-don't-need-it" defense of minimizing hazards has been attacked on the basis of the widespread use of chloramphenicol.

"We trust the drug companies. They wouldn't lie to us," says Dr. Virginia Ramirez de Barquero of the department of drugs in Costa Rica's Ministry of Public Health. But she also expresses her dismay at the way in which chloramphenicol products have been recommended for what are clearly trivial infections.

Some spokesmen for the multinational pharmaceutical companies have explained that physicians in the Latin American countries use the descriptions published in the reference books only as brief reminders, or summaries, of what may or may not be included in a package insert accompanying each shipment of drugs. But these package inserts may or may not be biased. They may not be read or even seen by a physician, and they are not readily filed for immediate reference. In the introduction to an authoritative drug guide in Venezuela, Dr. Marcel Granier-Doyeux has written:

> The need of the practicing physician to keep himself continually informed about pharmaceutical specialties is unquestionable. Now this information is not found even in the pharmacopoeias, nor in the national formularies, nor in the pharmacology or therapeutics texts. On the other hand, the pamphlets of 'propaganda' distributed by the commercial enterprises are far from fulfilling that informational end. . . . How often does it happen that the propaganda pamphlet ends up in

the wastepaper basket? The immediate consequence is that this information is never at hand at the precise moment when it is most needed.[3]

In some Latin American cities, physicians report they are accustomed to visits from a detail man, a *visitador*, who will give a brief presentation on his company's products and then point to a copy of the *Diccionario* he is carrying — or to the copy on the physician's bookshelf — and say, "All the information you need is in that book."

It is similarly argued that adequate information on hazards is given to the physician by the detail man. Therefore, when the promotional material from the Latin American works was translated from Spanish or Portuguese into English — these translations formed the basis of the tables presented in the preceding seven chapters — drafts were submitted to each pharmaceutical company to assure that no errors had been made in the translating. (Of the twenty-one companies concerned, seventeen graciously replied and made whatever technical corrections were necessary.) Several company officials commented that the Latin American volumes do not represent government-approved material and thus do not have the same status as *PDR* in the United States. The vice president and medical director of one major firm made these comments:

> Our policy in Latin America, as it is everywhere in the world, is to communicate information consistent with available scientific data, to enable physicians to use our products properly and safely. This is essential to the ethical conduct of our business. . . . The most important source of [the company's] product information for physicians in Latin America is our sales representatives, who regularly visit prescribing physicians, informing them of the proper and safe uses of our products. . . .

But in Latin America as in the United States, it is commonly said that "you don't expect a salesman to knock his own product."

In virtually every Latin American country, before a product can be approved and licensed for marketing, the company must file a complete description, in which a full disclosure of hazards is supposedly required. If a physician is willing, he can visit the ministry of health and consult the official records. But some physicians have complained that obtaining access to these official papers is often a difficult and time-consuming procedure, and on some occasions the files have been misplaced.

In some instances, the drug descriptions in the Latin American reference books contain a statement that more complete instructions on prescribing can be obtained by consulting a monograph available from the manufacturer. It is not known how often physicians avail themselves of such information sources. Further, it would seem that physicians should not have the responsibility for requesting such material; instead, especially when contraindications and warnings are concerned, it should be legally required that the manufacturer has the responsibility to keep physicians informed in all promotional material.

Frequently, emphasis is placed on the argument that it is not in the best interests of a drug manufacturer to mislead physicians, or government officials, and that what is involved is an honest difference of opinion or a controversy among medical experts themselves. "This argument would be more palatable," says a Colombian health official, "if the company would tell one story in the United States, where there are strict FDA rules, and another throughout Latin America, where perhaps the rules are less formidable. But when we find the company tells one story here in Bogotá, another in Quito, another in Brasilia, and still another in Mexico City, that is difficult to comprehend."

Occasionally it has been claimed that there is no valid reason for the health authorities in Latin American countries to follow the policies and decisions of FDA. "These authorities are not under the jurisdiction of the United States Food and Drug Administration," the board chairman of Warner-Lambert (which now includes both Parke-Davis and Warner-Chilcott) told a meeting of stockholders, "nor do they necessarily believe the Food and Drug Administration is the foremost authority on drugs for the local health problems of every nation."[4]

But Dr. George Rosenkranz, head of Syntex in Mexico City, and a distinguished steroid chemist, comments:

> This is only partially true. FDA cannot be viewed simply as a United States agency. In health ministries throughout Latin America and Western Europe, more often than not it *is* looked upon as the foremost governmental authority on drugs. Its decisions, even though they are not binding outside the U.S., serve as invaluable guidelines throughout the world. In Europe, and here in the Americas, it is common for health officials to tell a United States drug company, 'It would be much easier for us to approve your product in our country if it was already approved in the United States. And if your product is as good as you claim, why hasn't the FDA approved it?'[5]

The unreasonableness of expecting a global organization to behave like a monolithic structure is sometimes stressed. It should be expected that a policy enunciated in Manhattan, London, Paris, Tokyo, Frankfurt, or even Moscow may be more or less modified to meet conditions in different countries. This obviously is true with such entities as General Motors, DuPont, Dow Chemical, the major oil companies, and the leading world banks. This apparent lack of a consistent international policy may, in fact, be company policy.[6]

For the multinational pharmaceutical companies, it seems to be expected that local managers are knowledgeable citizens of the countries in which they work and that they will modify instructions from headquarters as necessary to meet local conditions. As one promotional expert in Ecuador puts it, "This is simply an accepted idea of good business. You don't necessarily adopt any company policy if, in your country, it will put you at a competitive disadvantage." What this means, at least in some cases, is that a product may be promoted in a particular Latin American country not simply on the basis of scientific evidence but to meet the claims being made for a competitive product. "If your competitor isn't disclosing the serious side effects of his product, it's economically suicidal for you to disclose the hazards of yours."

Company representatives in Latin America appear to be convinced that using moderation in their claims of efficacy or warning physicians of potential hazards would undoubtedly reduce the sales of their products. Accordingly, if their company's profit structure is to be preserved and funds are to continue to be siphoned back to headquarters for distribution to stockholders, the sales to Latin American patients will need to be raised — or, in the standard gambit long used by drug companies when any governmental control measure is proposed, the claim is made that "we'll just have to cut down on our research."

It has long been known that these attitudes and policies — or nonpolicies — have been the subject of bitter dispute at the highest levels of some United States-based drug companies. In these internal battles, the company's research or medical directors have found themselves most often pitted against those concerned primarily with sales, profits, and dividends.

"For years," says a former vice-president for research in one major pharmaceutical firm, who did not wish to be identified, "I tried to convince our people that we must say the same things for our products in every country where we sold them. Anything else is unconscionable. But I failed. Whenever I insisted we clean up our promotional materials, my proposal was vetoed by one of our local managers in Tokyo, or Madrid, or Buenos Aires, or Guatemala City."

Ironically, after this official resigned from his frustrating position, his company, along with two or three others, announced they would start in 1973 or 1974 to present the same indications and warnings in every country. But because of what were described as "publishing difficulties," it was not expected that significant changes would be visible before 1975 or 1976.

Finally, for at least the past decade, spokesmen for the major global drug companies have defended the all-too-obvious discrepancies in their drug promotion by stating that their actions were completely legal — "We're not breaking any laws." For example, Warner-Lambert stockholders were told: "Having taken these extensive measures and considering that Warner-Lambert's foreign affiliates are guests of the host country, and that most of these affiliates are managed by nationals of that country, Warner-Lambert believes that it has fully lived up to both its corporate, social and humanitarian responsibility and to the laws and procedures of foreign governments."[7]

"We're Not Breaking Any Laws"

Company stockholders and members of U.S. Senate investigating committees exposed to such sentiments were apparently in no position to question them. Copies of foreign drug laws are not readily available in most public libraries in the United States, or in most foreign embassies in Washington, D.C., or for that matter even in some health ministries in the foreign nations themselves.

During 1974, it became possible for me to conduct on-site investigations in most of the Latin American countries concerned here and to obtain copies of the pertinent drug laws. An examination of these materials and consultations with Latin American health officials and attorneys showed:

— In some countries, the drug company statements were apparently true. No laws or regulations were being violated. No pertinent laws were in existence.

— In others, the situation was different. It was evident that governmental health agencies had been given legal authority to require full disclosure of hazards to all physicians but, for whatever the reason, had not elected to apply their authority.

— In still other countries, company assertions of innocence were apparently not true. The medical promotion was in violation of laws requiring the disclosure of hazards.

Mexico. Government authorities have the power to "determine for which drugs the statements on indications, contraindications, undesirable side effects, and dosages must be shown in the labels, the package inserts, or the medical or public promotion."[8] According to Dr. Armando Bejarano, in charge of drug control in the Ministry of Health and Welfare, the regulation has never been applied in full force. The drug manufacturer is obliged to inform the government of all potential hazards but does not have to disclose this information in its promotional materials to physicians.

Costa Rica. A somewhat similar situation exists in Costa Rica, where "all deceitful or ambiguous advertising and promotion which can be prejudicial to public health is prohibited."[9] The law requires each manufacturer to submit in advance to the Ministry of Health the text of any proposed information or advertising. The power to require full disclosure of hazards, however, has rarely if ever been applied.

Nicaragua. There is apparently no national law requiring full disclosure to physicians, but the manufacturer must submit to health authorities the text of all proposed promotion.[10]

Guatemala. It appears there is no specific law requiring full disclosure of side effects to physicians, although attorney Arturo Lara Larrave of the Ministry of Health feels his agency does have the necessary authority to establish such a requirement.

Honduras and Panama. A 1969 tabulation of Central American drug legislation notes that disclosure of contraindications is legally required in both countries.[11]

El Salvador. The law specifies that contraindications must be included in the label or literature on each product.[12]

Colombia. Here the situation seems beyond question: the failure of pharmaceutical companies to disclose serious side effects in the reference books is clearly in violation of the law. In the National Health Code, it is stated:

> In the labels of the products [including all prescription drugs], there must be included name of the products, number of license, dosage and manner of use, contraindications, name of producing laboratory, and sales price to the public.[13]

A 1963 law contains the following:

> In the text of propaganda, whatever the medium used, in the literature to the medical profession, in the labels, in the package, and in the literature or package inserts accompanying the drugs which are not in official pharmacopoeias . . . there should always appear the contraindications, secondary effects, and precautions for use. The therapeutic indications, if any, shall be limited to those authorized by the respective license.[14]

Practically, however, these laws have never been enforced.

A 1964 decree assigns to the Office of Drug Control in the Ministry of Public Health "the approval of methods, presentations, and text of the propaganda for all drugs for human and animal use."[15] Dr. Gustavo Hitzig Berggrun, head of the Office of Drug Control, says, "We have not seriously applied legal controls on what a drug company must say to physicians. We have not required full listings of contraindications and warnings." Dr. José Félix Patiño, an internationally known authority on medical education, executive director of the Panamerican Federation of Associations of Medical Schools, and former Minister of Health, adds: "Here in Colombia, the laws are not strong — certainly not as strong as those in the United States — and unfortunately the enforcement is even weaker. Drug companies can afford to take a chance. If they're caught, they risk only a small fine."†

Ecuador. The manufacturer must submit all proposed publicity and advertising to the government but is not required to disclose to physicians any information on hazards.[16]

Brazil. National laws do not require full disclosure of contraindications, warnings, or side effects in all promotional material.[17]

Argentina. There are apparently no laws requiring full disclosure to physicians of adverse drug reactions or other hazards.

In those countries which do have drug promotion laws that have not been enforced, and in those which have the authority to write strong regulations but have not acted, it would be unjust to saddle health officials with much blame. With the enormous worldwide influence of multinational corporations on legislatures and administrative agencies, and the skill of their legal and public relations staffs, it may be unreasonable to demand that health officials undertake enforcement campaigns that would be time-consuming, costly far beyond their budgetary capabilities, and possibly thwarted by powerful interests within their own governments. As Barnet and Müller have declared, the power of governments over multinational corporations in the developing nations is exceedingly weak and ineffective.[18] The effect of possible drug industry nationalization in such countries in the future is not clear.

†Early in 1975, Alfonso Lopez Michelson, President of the Republic, and Dr. Haroldo Calvo Nuñez, Minister of Health, signed a new decree providing even more stringent controls over drug promotion. In Decree 284, Article 22, it is stated that all information on drugs directed to physicians, veterinarians, and dentists must be approved in advance by the Ministry of Public Health. Article 27 states: "In the information or advertising to physicians, veterinarians, and dentists, it is required that the contraindications, secondary or side effects, risks of administration, teratological effects, pharmacogenetic problems, risks of pharmacodependency, and other precautions or warnings be specified, *without omitting any which are described in the scientific literature or which are known to the manufacturer*." [Italics ours.] Further emphasis appears in Article 30: "The advertising or information to physicians, veterinarians, and dentists must conform to scientific truth and to the standards set by the Ministry of Public Health and must show the favorable as well as the unfavorable aspects of the medication." (*El Tiempo*, Bogotá, February 23, 1975, p. 1)

In most Latin American countries, laws require that any drug product imported from a foreign nation must have been approved for marketing in the "country of origin." With this "country of origin" rule, it has puzzled some observers to find that certain products originally introduced in the United States but later taken off the market by FDA orders—for example, fixed-ratio antibiotic products—can continue to be imported and sold in Latin America. The solution has been simple: the United States-based corporation needs only to set up a plant to produce the drug—or merely to put it in finished dosage form (not in the United States but in Nation X), manage to get it approved by the obliging Nation X authorities, and then ship it throughout Latin America with Nation X listed as the official "country of origin." A similar device has been used by some European companies with drugs that had to be withdrawn from the European market as ineffective or excessively dangerous.

Concerning Socioeconomic Factors

In any country, the marketing, promotion, use, and misuse of drug products may be significantly influenced by social or moral standards, religious attitudes, educational levels, individual or national purchasing power, the extent of poverty, the accessibility of physicians and the fees they charge, and the prevalence of certain diseases. Economic factors may determine whether a Latin American patient will seek a prescription from a physician or go directly to a pharmacist, or even obtain medicine from a village *brujo* (witch doctor). Economic factors may likewise influence the societal or political decision to approve a drug that is widely applicable and less expensive but far more dangerous than another. In some cultures, the rights and needs of the individual are generally considered to be paramount; in others the rights and needs of society carry more weight.

"In a poor country like Mexico," says Dr. Javier Robles Gil of Mexico's National Institute of Cardiology, "it is very bad when the breadwinner of a family gets sick. To get such a man back to work quickly, many physicians take a chance and prescribe a treatment that is a little dangerous. But if the patient is away from work too long, his wife and children may go hungry."

Such factors as these are evidently involved in the ways in which oral contraceptives are promoted in Latin America and their potential side effects glossed over. In these countries, with predominantly Catholic populations, it might be expected that these drugs would be recommended for such socially inoffensive uses as the control of premenstrual tension, menstrual pain, and menopausal problems—uses not approved in the United States—and that their value as contraceptives would be minimized or not mentioned. Actually, as reported in Chapter 3, all of the products are described clearly and openly as contraceptive or anovulatory agents.

Less emphasis is placed on the potential dangers of oral contraceptives. This is not an unexpected situation. In countries with rapidly increasing populations, serious poverty, widespread malnutrition, lack of educational facilities, inadequate numbers of physicians, and both pregnant women and infants at relatively high risk, the use of these products may be approved under conditions not acceptable in other nations.

"We don't say much about the need for a woman to have a regular Pap smear while she's using The Pill," says a Mexican health expert. "She's far less worried about the risk of cancer than getting that sixth, or eighth, or tenth baby."

In many Latin American countries, family-planning programs have been developing so rapidly that there are not enough physicians to explain all the uncommon but possibly serious hazards of The Pill. In many areas, it is the pharmacist who prescribes and dispenses the contraceptives, and some obstetricians foresee the time when the drugs will be commonly dispensed by quickly trained nonprofessionals.

"With so many people giving out oral contraceptives," says one gynecologist, "it is probably unreasonable to demand that every woman should be given all the warnings, or that she get a routine Pap smear. Few countries would have the money or the manpower to undertake such a job. But this is a decision which each country must make for itself."

Yet another cultural aspect is concerned if a physician in Latin America makes an unscientific decision, if he prescribes irrationally, and the patient is seriously harmed.

"Everywhere in Latin America," says Dr. Silvestre Frenk, director of the famed Hospital de Pediatria of the Mexican Institute of Social

Security, "it is unthinkable for anyone to sue a doctor for malpractice. Physicians in these countries do not carry malpractice insurance. Most of them don't even know what it is. Further, if a company markets a product that injures or kills people, seldom if ever is it sued for damages."[19]

Of Prices and Profits

Foreign drug sales by global drug companies can no longer be considered a minor item. For U.S.-based corporations, annual domestic sales rose from $1.5 billion in 1955 to $1.9 billion in 1960, $2.8 billion in 1965, $4.3 billion in 1970, and an estimated $6.5 billion in 1974, an increase of 333 percent during nearly two decades. Foreign sales skyrocketed from $0.4 billion in 1955 to $1.0 billion in 1960, $1.4 billion in 1965, $2.5 billion in 1970, and an estimated $5.0 billion in 1974, an increase of over 1000 percent.[20] It may be predicted that, barring a worldwide economic collapse, foreign sales will soon match domestic sales. Many of these foreign sales by U.S. corporations went to countries in Europe, Asia, and Africa, but a substantial portion went to Latin American nations.

The prices charged for these drugs in foreign markets are as difficult to explain as the different promotional claims. For example, it was reported in 1967 that the list price to pharmacists for one hundred 0.25-mg tablets of CIBA's Serpasil was $4.50 in the United States, $3.00 in Mexico, $1.60 in Brazil, $1.24 in Switzerland, and $1.05 in West Germany.[21] Schering's Meticorten was listed at $17.90 for one hundred 5-mg tablets in the United States, $22.70 in Canada, $12.26 in Mexico, $5.30 in Brazil, and $4.37 in Switzerland.[22]

A 1971 report on retail prices for the same quantities of selected drug products showed comparable inconsistencies in the United States, Brazil, and other countries.[23]

Attempts by drug company officials and others to rationalize these and similar price differences have resulted only in confusion. In some cases it was argued that the lower prices were set in certain foreign countries because of their poverty, lower standard of living, and lower purchasing power, or because of differences in living costs, wage scales, taxes, size of markets, attempts to forestall inflation, and currency problems. None of these satisfactorily explained why, for example, Serpasil was priced at $3.00 in Mexico and $1.05 in affluent West Germany.

From the floundering but unsuccessful attempts to find any other convincing explanation, it is conceivable that the widely different international prices are often set on a more elemental basis: they are the highest that the traffic will bear.

While Senator Gaylord Nelson and others have focused their attention on low prices charged in foreign countries — presumably yielding handsome profits nonetheless — and demanded that the drug companies set the same prices in the United States, others have emphasized the overpricing of drugs in Latin America.[24] In their book *Global Reach*, Barnet and Müller cite surveys revealing that, in Latin America, global corporations — where it is to their overall advantage — "wildly overvalue" their imports. "Over-pricing imports and under-pricing exports are good ways to repatriate more profits than the local government allows," they say. "All of this makes good business sense, but its impact on the economy of poor countries is cruel."[25]

Whether there is over-pricing or under-pricing, these foreign sales are generally profitable. For at least some U.S.-based companies, the profit rate on foreign sales is higher than that on sales within the United States. According to Barnet and Müller, the average reported profit of the pharmaceutical industry as based on net worth was 15.5 percent from operations in the United States and 22.4 percent from foreign operations.[26] Net profits, as based on net worth, and on sales after payment of all taxes, research costs, and all other expenses, for eleven selected companies in the year 1974 are indicated in the table on the opposite page.

Of Doctors, Detail Men, and Druggists

It is possible to consider the physicians of practically every country in the Americas in two broad categories.

One consists of those working in or closely associated with a major medical center. Most of them have been highly trained, and many have taken postgraduate training in the United States or Europe. They read the world's leading medical journals. They have access to good libraries, and they make use of them. They attend national and

Net Profits on U.S. and Foreign Operations
of Selected Major Drug Companies, 1974

Company	Profits (%) Based on Net Worth		Profits (%) Based on Sales	
	U.S.	Foreign	U.S.	Foreign
Eli Lilly	16.7	39.6	17.0	14.7
Merck	24.9	26.5	15.9	15.8
Miles Laboratories	14.8	7.8[a]	4.1	4.1
Pfizer	11.8	19.2	6.1	11.1
Rorer-Amchem	20.0	23.9	10.8[b]	14.3[b]
Schering-Plough	21.1	34.1	19.2	15.6
Smith Kline & French	24.5	9.5	13.9	4.6
Squibb	17.0	13.8	7.8	10.9
Sterling Drug	16.7	17.9[c]	8.7	9.3[c]
Upjohn	16.4	18.2	8.7	8.7
Warner-Lambert	27.4[d]	26.5[d]	14.4[d]	12.9[d]

SOURCE: "Foreign Profit Performance," *Business International,* August 22, 1975, p. 269.
[a]Based on total equity in international operations
[b]Sales include royalties and other technical fees
[c]Excludes the accounts of all subsidiaries located in South America
[d]Based on pre-tax earnings

international scientific meetings. Their offices are equipped with excellent textbooks. They consult frequently with their peers and maintain communications with colleagues in other countries. Many refuse to see drug company representatives or read drug advertising. They are distressed by the problem of irrational drug prescribing and drug misuse. It seems apparent that, in most cases, the quality of medicine they practice, in such cities as Mexico City, Bogotá, or Rio de Janeiro, is as high as that practiced by their opposite numbers in Boston, New York, or San Francisco.

In the other group are physicians who have little or no contact with medical schools or other centers. Few have taken any postgraduate studies. They rarely read medical journals and have limited or no access to adequate medical libraries. They do not generally attend scientific meetings, and they infrequently consult with their colleagues. Their chief sources of information are drug company promotion and the presentations of detail men. Many of them practice in small villages, but there are also many working in large cities. They are apparently unaware of any problem of irrational prescribing, or strongly deny that their own prescribing judgments may be irrational. The quality of the care they provide in Latin America is probably as low as that which can be observed in some areas of the United States.

"These are second-class physicians practicing second-class medicine," says Dr. Jorge Espino Vela, director of the National Institute of Cardiology in Mexico City. "Our big failure lies in not educating many physicians adequately and then keeping them up to date. Too often, their only link to knowledge is the detail man."

In San José, Dr. Fernando Montero Gei, dean of Costa Rica's School of Biology, declares, "Too many doctors in rural areas, and even in the cities, stop learning when they graduate. They do not learn from journals or books or their peers. Their only source of information, or misinformation, is the drug company representative."

The temptation for a competent general practitioner to find work elsewhere, preferably in the United States, is considerable. With the exception of a relatively few specialists, in most Latin American countries a physician can expect to earn not much more than $6,000 or $7,000 a year.

Detail Men. The situation for detail men, or *visitadores*, is far different. In the United States, there are estimated to be about 24,000 company representatives who call periodically on some 250,000 practicing physicians, a ratio of one detail man to about ten doctors. In Ecuador, there are 440 detail men for 3,500 physicians, a ratio of one detail man to about eight. In Colombia, there are 2,200 detail men for 11,500 physicians, one to five. There are 650 detail men to about 2,000 physicians in Guatemala, roughly 9,000 detail men for 32,000 physicians in Mexico, and 14,100 detail men for 45,000 practicing physicians in Brazil—in these three countries, a ratio of approximately one to three.

In these countries, the average detail man makes a bigger income, part salary and part commission, than does the average physician.

What has aroused the ire of medical men is not merely that most *visitadores* are better paid but that most of them know little about their products and have been trained primarily to make a smooth, persuasive sales presentation.

"The *visitadores*," says Dr. Frenk in Mexico City, "are sort of 'traveling professors of therapeutics.' While some medical men refuse to take their advice, most doctors take advice only from them. In most of Latin America, they have completed only a secondary education. They give a smooth, technically sounding sales argument which they have memorized. If you ask them a question in the middle of their talk, they may have to go all the way back to the beginning to start again. They give you their company 'literature.' They may give you reprints of published articles which extol their products, but they tell you nothing about the articles which question the efficacy of those products or expose their dangers."[27]

Says Dr. Hitzig Berggrun of Colombia's Ministry of Health, "In this country, the physician is in the hands of the detail men. They brainwash him."[28]

Also in Colombia, Dr. Patiño says, "The situation here is very bad. Communication with our medical people is inadequate. We cannot reach them. It is the company representative, the *visitador*, who tells them how to prescribe. It is shocking to realize that the salesman has, in fact, become the prescriber."[29]

In few countries are government officials moving to alter this situation. A new law in Costa Rica, however, has given the Ministry of Health the authority to require that detail men now working can continue to hold their positions, but in the future all new *visitadores* must have a degree in pharmacy or medicine.

As one partial antidote to biased or incomplete presentations by detail men or other drug promotion, a Spanish version of the prestigious U.S. publication *The Medical Letter* is now being distributed to several thousand physicians in some Latin American countries. Published by an independent nonprofit organization in the United States, *The Medical Letter* contains evaluations written by highly qualified drug specialists on the effectiveness, safety, and relative value of various drug products. It contains no drug advertising. Since 1965, through arrangements with governmental or private nonprofit agencies involved in medical education in Latin America, each biweekly issue of *The Medical Letter* is published in Spanish as *Carta Medica* and made available to sponsoring organizations for distribution without charge to physicians. The sponsor remits to *The Medical*

Letter the sum of 50¢ per year for each physician, in payment for the authorized translation and editorial rights for its reproduction. Currently about 6,000 copies are being sent regularly to physicians in Colombia, Guatemala, Panama, and Ecuador.[30] This circulation would represent approximately 30 percent of the physicians practicing in those countries. (Copies are also distributed to physicians in Peru.) As valuable as *Carta Medica* may be as a source of objective information, however, it is not intended to be a complete reference work on all or even most drugs.

Druggists. In the Latin American countries, the pharmacist occupies a peculiarly strategic position. In rural areas and small villages, he may be the only health professional available. It is against the law for him to diagnose and to prescribe so-called prescription drugs, but in most instances — except for morphine and other narcotics, and perhaps for some psychoactive agents — he dispenses without requiring any prescription, in the firm belief that "the government looks the other way."

In the cities, too, the pharmacist occupies a similar key position. Many patients are eligible for free treatment by a physician under a national social security program, but too often the patient must wait all day, or many days, to see such a physician. The patient can go to a private physician, but he must pay a fee — sometimes $2 or more — which in many cases he cannot afford. Accordingly, the patient goes directly to a pharmacist, describes his symptoms, and buys whatever remedy the pharmacist recommends.

In some jungle areas, and other remote districts, not even a pharmacist is available, and the patient will go for help to a witch doctor. The *brujo* may dispense a concoction of herbs which may or may not be effective. Or he may give the patient a packet of capsules or tablets containing a highly active prescription drug. How the *brujo* obtains his supplies of these drugs, whether from a pharmacist in a distant city or a company detail man, is not clear.

The competence of some Latin American pharmacists has been seriously questioned by medical experts. At Costa Rica's Hospital San Juan de Dios, Dr. Victor Mario Rodriguez Ancheta says, "When we ask a pharmacist why he sold a particularly dangerous drug to a patient without a prescription — a patient who later suffered a severe or fatal drug reaction—his defense is, 'If I didn't give the lady what she wanted, she would only have gone to another pharmacy.' And when we ask a pharmacist why he sold a patient only a one-day supply of an antibiotic, when it is essential to use the drug for at least a week, he tells us, 'She had only the money to buy enough for one day.'"

Physicians in Ecuador complain that if a pharmacist receives a prescription for a specific antibiotic such as tetracycline but has no tetracycline in stock, he will substitute another antibiotic, like chloramphenicol, without bothering to notify the doctor. Such a substitution is illegal in the United States and most European countries, and it rarely occurs.

Throughout Latin America, it is considered a rarity for a pharmacist to ask a patient about any known drug allergies. Patients known to be sensitive to penicillin, for example, have been given penicillin on the advice of a pharmacist, and some have died of an allergic reaction.

The problem of irrational and also illegal diagnosing, prescribing, and dispensing by pharmacists will not be readily solved. The education of pharmacists and the quality and quantity of information supplied to them could be improved to minimize dangerously irrational prescribing by them, but this would mean continuing to condone violations of the laws which say that a pharmacist should not prescribe a prescription drug in the first place. On the other hand, such laws could be enforced more vigorously to halt or at least minimize illegal prescribing by pharmacists. But if simultaneous steps were not taken to provide more ready access to more physicians, at a cost that most patients could readily afford to pay, this tightened enforcement would probably represent only an overall disservice to the patients.

In Colombia, Dr. Hitzig Berggrun estimates that there are now about 7,000 licensed pharmacists, but only some 1,500 of them are graduates of a pharmacy school. "The others," he says, "only had to show they spent ten years as a pharmacist's assistant or clerk and are of good moral character."

Many physicians, especially those in medical centers, express the belief that most pharmacists are not adequately trained. "But this may not be as important as the fact that few of them spend much time with patients," one physician says. "Most of their work is done for them by even less well trained assistants."

An example of how such a pharmacist assistant may function is an incident we witnessed in one of the largest pharmacies in Costa Rica:

> A middle-aged woman, thin, haggard, and jittery, described her symptoms — highly suggestive of hyperthyroidism — to a white-coated assistant and asked for a specific tranquilizer. The assistant said, "I have something better for you." Without consulting anyone, he took from a shelf behind him a bottle of a powerful antithyroid drug, so potent that physicians in the United States are advised that it should be given only under the most careful supervision of a physician and preferably while the patient is hospitalized. The patient bought the recommended product. What made this incident unforgettable is that we were uncertain whether the pharmacist's assistant was aged 12, 13, or 14.

The Prices Patients Pay

The fact that some global pharmaceutical companies are bending or breaking drug promotion laws in Latin America is one aspect of irrational drug use or misuse. The fact that many physicians and pharmacists are seemingly uninformed or misinformed is another. Most important is the resulting impact on Latin American patients.

In this connection, chloramphenicol has attracted particular attention. In 1973, Michael Dunne and his colleagues in London reported a survey of chloramphenicol labeling in twenty-one countries — no Latin American countries were included — and revealed remarkable differences in the listing of indications and the disclosures of hazards.[31] Among the surveyed countries was Egypt, where a multitude of recommended uses were listed but possible blood or bone-marrow effects were not mentioned. More recently, a team of investigators in Cairo reported that — perhaps as a result of such promotion — chloramphenicol was administered to 86 of 129 patients hospitalized with "fever of unknown origin": 57 of 78 with infections, 11 of 18 with malignancies, 7 of 13 with collagen diseases, and 11 of 20 suffering from other illnesses.[32]

"In nearly every case chloramphenicol was the physician's first choice, and only when there was no response were other antibiotics used," the Egyptian team said. Under the circumstances, it was not astonishing that chloramphenicol-resistant strains of paratyphoid organisms appeared on the wards.

The widespread use of chloramphenicol as "a daily self-medication for all ills and aches" in a Latin American country such as Colombia has long been apparent. One physician declared that use of this kind without a report of any significant occurrence of aplastic anemia was an indication that the natives of the country are protected, perhaps by some genetic factor, against this blood dyscrasia.[33] But another Colombian physician retorted that the occurrence of aplastic anemia following chloramphenicol therapy is neither nonexistent nor rare. In a four-year period, he said in a letter to the *New England Journal of Medicine*, dozens of cases were documented, with a mortality rate of 60 percent. "Diseases supposedly 'rare' in South America, but common in other countries," he wrote, "usually make their appearance as soon as somebody starts looking for them."[34] Another physician stated, "Indeed, it is agreed by all Colombia hematologists that as soon as chloramphenicol became freely available in this country, the expected occurred—that is, aplastic anemia became a dreadfully common disease."[35]

In late 1974, some Latin American physicians expressed their opinion that chloramphenicol-induced aplastic anemia was becoming less frequent — "Thank God!" one said. "Maybe the drug is going out of fashion!" — but others felt the situation was still serious.

"When a child is given chloramphenicol for typhoid fever, and it dies from aplastic anemia," says Dr. Rubén Mayorga, former dean of the School of Microbiology in Guatemala City, "this is a tragedy but perhaps an unavoidable tragedy. But where it happens when the drug is used to treat a case of virus pneumonia, or an undiagnosed upper respiratory infection, or a sore throat, this is unconscionable."

After one patient died from aplastic anemia following chloramphenicol given for tonsillitis, a small-town physician was asked, "Why in the name of heaven did you use this drug for such a trivial infection? Didn't you know such a thing could happen?"

The physician replied, "No, I did not know. Nobody warned me."

At the National Institute of Nutrition in Mexico City, Dr. Luis Sánchez Medal and his associates have reported that Mexico has what seems to be an exceptionally high rate of fatal aplastic anemia, a finding that may be related to the large proportion of susceptible Indians in the population. One out of every 1,000 patients admitted for forty-eight hours or more to four pediatric hospitals in Mexico City was suffering from aplastic anemia. Many of these cases seemed related to overexposure to insecticides, but a substantial portion were associated with chloramphenicol. In his own series of such patients, 30 percent died within two months after diagnosis.[36],[37]

Chloramphenicol is by no means the only drug implicated in these serious or fatal drug reactions. Medical experts cite life-threatening blood dyscrasias caused by the irrational use of phenylbutazone and similar antiarthritic products, lethal reactions following use of dangerous antibiotics like amphotericin B without adequate supervision and sometimes without even a definite diagnosis, and the explosive flare-ups of tuberculosis, candidiasis, and other infections after prolonged use of steroids.

"They're dispensing these corticosteroids as if they were aspirin," declares Dr. Mayorga.

In Mexico City, Dr. Frenk says, "Many of the serious or fatal adverse reactions we see here are the result of self-medication, without the involvement of any physician. But irrational prescribing by physicians is all too evident, and the damage done is tragically obvious."

Dr. Alfonso Trejos Willis, at Costa Rica's Hospital San Juan de Dios, says, "Out in the country, some patients don't go to a doctor or a pharmacist. They go to a witch doctor. That may be safer."

Concerning Corporate Ethics

One of the traditional and most cherished defenses of drug company promotion has been based on the concept that few if any such corporations would engage in unethical activities—like exaggerating claims for their products or failing to make full disclosure of hazards— because such reprehensible actions would cost them the trust and confidence of physicians.

This view has been expressed particularly well by George Teeling-Smith, one of the most highly regarded drug experts in Great Britain:

> Before discussing the ethics of pharmaceutical sales promotion in detail, it would perhaps be useful to make a more general observation, namely the twin myths that commercial ethics are in some way inferior to standards of morality in other spheres of life and that the so-called profit motive is responsible for this situation . . .

[C]oncern now centres on the risk that pharmaceutical manufacturers may be tempted to make excessive claims to persuade doctors to prescribe the company's medicines in cases where they would not in reality be necessary or effective. Thus, it is suggested that a manufacturer may attempt to increase his sales and profits by encouraging the use of his preparations in cases where some other remedy—or perhaps none at all—would have been preferable. . . . There are, however, many safeguards to prevent such over-enthusiastic selling . . .

At one extreme, there is frank and wholly intentional misrepresentation. Next there is obviously misguided over-enthusiasm for the benefits of a medicine and suppression of its disadvantages. Finally, there is the genuine difference of opinion, occurring in good faith and based on equally sincere judgements on the two sides . . .

If a manager or representative is concerned with the development of his business or his sales for anything more than a few months ahead, it is against his own interests for prescribers to have their faith in his preparations undermined. . . .

In contrast to the deliberate wrongdoers, an incompetent manager in one company may fail to understand clearly or refuse to admit to himself the limitations of his products or may seriously misjudge the risks associated with them. If the claims he makes for his products are unjustifiable he will once again do his firm harm by undermining confidence in it, and hence act against his own long term interest.[38]

It is quite possible that this situation exists in the United Kingdom. It most certainly is not true for the United States. In the United States, the situation may be demonstrated, for example, by the remarkable case of MER/29, a drug promoted on the basis of what was later shown to be criminally fraudulent evidence of safety. The manufacturing company and three of its officials were found guilty in Federal courts. Injured victims sued and collected tens of millions of dollars in damages. Certainly no "honest difference of opinion" was involved. Yet, although this entire story was widely reported, the company continued to maintain the confidence of physicians, and its sales and profits continued to rise.[39] Other companies found to be engaged in playing down the hazards of their products were similarly spared any significant loss of confidence, even when they were obliged to retract their claims in "Dear Doctor" letters written to every practicing physician in the nation.[40] Perhaps, in the United States, physicians have a shorter memory or a more forgiving nature.

In a consideration of the ethics of science in 1965, Dr. Bentley Glass of the State University of New York at Stony Brook developed these four "commandments" of science:[41],[42]

1. Cherish complete truthfulness.

2. Avoid self-aggrandizement at the expense of one's fellow scientist.

3. Fearlessly defend the freedom of scientific inquiry and opinion.

4. Fully communicate one's findings through primary publication, synthesis, and instruction.

Emerging from those commandments, he said, are "the social and ethical responsibilities of scientists that in the past 20 years have begun to loom ever larger in our ken." He grouped these responsibilities as follows:

1. the proclamations of benefits;

2. the warning of risks; and

3. the discussion of quandaries.

More recently, Dr. Van R. Potter of the University of Wisconsin commented on such responsibilities and said:

> As scientists we have witnessed not only the most blatant examples of questionable advertising ethics in the fields of non-prescription drugs, cosmetics, detergents, and foods, but even in the case of prescription drugs . . . [M]embers of the pharmaceutical industry have definitely exceeded propriety by advocating that physicians prescribe tranquilizers and energizers for all sorts of common social interactions in a plain attempt to widen the area of presumed deviation from normality. What do the four commandments advise the individual scientist to do about this situation? It appears that they have permitted widespread apathy. I suggest that individuals act by urging their professional societies to publicize the issues and recommend action.

In addition, Dr. Potter raised, but did not attempt to answer, this question: "What is the magnitude of the vested interests that minimize the extent of risks when money is involved?"[43]

Some pharmaceutical industry leaders have denied that their Latin American promotion is unethical in any way. As to their decision not to make full disclosure of all hazards, they insist they are not lying, that what they say is truthful and accurate.

But in Colombia, Dr. Patiño says, "Where drug companies are concerned, where life may be at stake, not telling lies is not enough. Not telling *all* the truth is not enough."

In addition, he says, "U.S. manufacturers would be put to shame if the U.S. public knew how they were promoting their products in Latin America."

It is appropriate to refer again to two noteworthy exceptions shown above: the relatively substantial disclosure of hazards published in some countries for Merck's Indocid and the substantial identity between the descriptions published in the United States and Mexico for Lilly's Aventyl. Merck officials say, "This may harm us competitively during a short term, but in the long run we will benefit." And a high-ranking research officer of Eli Lilly says, "Every pharmaceutical company doing international business must tell the truth, all the truth, in every country. We can't settle for less."

Of Social Responsibility

If only for humanitarian reasons, the world cannot condone deceit or truth-twisting in science, especially where health is at stake. It cannot tolerate the dissemination of biased, incomplete, or inaccurate information when the cost may be needless injury or death.

At the same time, neither the United States nor any other nation has a mandate or moral right to export its health policies to other countries, or to induce by whatever means any other country to adopt its own decisions, practices, customs, techniques, or standards. The health-policy decisions in each of the Latin American countries must be made by those countries. Any attempt by a foreign nation to play the role of Big Brother in Latin American policies would be unrealistic, impractical, and impertinent.

Certainly, it is unreasonable to expect Latin American countries to change their value systems to those of the United States or the United Kingdom, or any other nation, or to accept any assertions that their own value systems are inferior.

The role of the government of the United States in attempting to influence or control international activities of U.S.-based corporations is not clear. Although Congress has the constitutional power to control foreign and domestic commerce, there appears to be no simple technique to control the labeling of drugs manufactured or marketed abroad by a foreign subsidiary of a United States corporation. (It is significant that no way has yet been found to require that U.S. brands of cigarettes carry the so-called Surgeon General's warning when they are marketed in Latin America.) But the Congress of the United States does have the right, which it has utilized effectively before, to investigate and report its findings to the entire nation.

Where "corporate responsibility" is concerned, answers are needed to fundamental questions. Where does this "corporate responsibility" lie? Is it the responsibility to the company's officers, or its stockholders, or its customers — including those in foreign countries — or to the entire community, both national and international?

If only for enlightened self-interest, it would seem inescapable that corporate officials and their stockholders have the responsibility to assure that each multinational corporation bears its appropriate social responsibilities in every nation in which it operates.

It would seem equally inescapable that stockholders can no longer accept such excuses as "we're not breaking any laws," or "we're not telling any lies," or "we're not required to make full disclosure of dangers." When such practices are utilized to draw money out of an underdeveloped country, and patients are injured or killed, this is blood money indeed.

It is indisputable that the drugs involved are — or can be — invaluable agents to speed recovery from disease and prevent needless deaths. Where they are used properly, they have been a boon to mankind. The issue is not the benefits of their rational use but the drug labeling and promotion implicated in their dangerously irrational use.

Ready availability of full, unbiased information is an absolute essential for the practice of scientific medicine anywhere in the world. It is basic for the use of drugs with maximum benefits and minimum risks. Their use in any other manner is a violation of medical ethics. By supplying therapeutic agents to physicians and pharmacists, pharmaceutical companies participate in this drug use and, despite their profit motive, are likewise obliged to meet the ethical standards involved. To hide or gloss over hazards is contrary to this requirement. Whether or not a drug company failing to make full disclosure of risks is meeting legal requirements is only of secondary importance. The primary issue is whether or not the company is meeting ethical requirements. Laws and regulations do not establish the ethical obligation; instead, they merely specify it.

The record is all too clear that the judgment of what is or is not appropriate drug promotion cannot be left entirely to the global companies themselves, or necessarily to the U.S. Food and Drug Administration or any other single agency in any country. Here, it appears, action by a different group is warranted.

It is my strong belief that the international medical-scientific community has the unavoidable responsibility to assure—and not merely recommend—that full and objective information on drug products is made available to all nations in which they are marketed, *and to all health professionals—obviously including both physicians and pharmacists—who may prescribe or dispense.*

Because there always will be legitimate differences of opinion about the effectiveness and dangers of some drugs, and because one nation's standards need not apply universally, a group representing all interests should work to establish internationally applicable guidelines and minimum standards.

It is the responsibility of the world's medical-scientific community to determine which controversies over drug labeling and promotion represent "honest differences of opinion" and which represent unacceptable exaggeration of claims or minimizing of hazards.

It should be the responsibility of the world's medical-scientific community, along with the professional organizations of medical men and pharmacists in each country, to see that education in drug use—especially continuing postgraduate education—is constantly upgraded, and that programs of periodic recertification of physicians and pharmacists are developed.

In such activities, physicians and scientists in the United States have a right and an obligation to participate, not as spokesmen for the United States, but as members of the medical-scientific community.

It should also be the responsibility of the world's medical-scientific community to advise

—whether every physician and pharmacist in every country should be warned of adverse reactions that occur rarely or only of those that occur frequently;

—whether every physician and pharmacist in every country should be told about every possible adverse reaction or only those that may be serious or life-threatening;

—whether particularly hazardous drugs may be prescribed by any physician or only by one with special competence;

—whether certain drugs may be prescribed for any patient or only for one hospitalized or kept under constant medical supervision;

—whether those drugs removed from the market in any country as relatively unsafe or ineffective should be allowed on the market in any other nation, regardless of the "country of origin" clause.

The world's medical-scientific community has, of course, no formal structure. It is not composed of delegates officially appointed by their respective governments. It has no legal powers. But it is not without influence. This unofficial group has already played a key role in having controls placed on the use of human subjects in medical research, assuring more humane treatment of prisoners, reducing environmental pollution, slowing the worldwide population explosion, and placing safeguards on research in so-called genetic engineering.

Finally, it is—and probably should remain—the right of the individual physician in each country to determine with his patient how he will make use of the information made readily available to him. Only when he does have ready access to full and unbiased information can he treat his patients with the fewest possible risks and the greatest possible benefits.

That's what this book is all about.

REFERENCES

In the following pages, certain frequently cited references are abbreviated as
follows:

Goodman and Gilman = Louis S. Goodman and Alfred Gilman (eds.),
The Pharmacological Basis of Therapeutics (New York: Macmillan,
4th ed., 1970).

AMA Drug Evaluations = American Medical Association, Department
of Drugs, *AMA Drug Evaluations* (Acton, Mass.: Publishing Sciences
Group, 2nd ed., 1973).

Pills, Profits, and Politics = Milton Silverman and Philip R. Lee, *Pills,
Profits, and Politics* (Berkeley: University of California Press, 1974).

1. *Introduction*

1. Milton Silverman and Philip R. Lee, *Pills, Profits, and Politics*
(Berkeley: University of California Press, 1974), Chapters 3, 12.

2. Gaylord Nelson, statement in U.S. Senate, Select Committee on Small
Business, Subcommittee on Monopoly, *Present Status of Competition in the
Pharmaceutical Industry* (Washington, D.C.: U.S. Government Printing
Office, 1967) 6:2222.

3. *Physicians' Desk Reference* (Oradell, N.J.: Medical Economics, 1973).

4. Emilio Rosenstein, Alfonso Martín del Campo, and Ignacio Landero
(eds.), *Diccionario de Especialidades Farmacéuticas, Edición Mexicana*
(Mexico City: Ediciones PLM, 20th ed., 1973).

5. Emilio Rosenstein and Alfonso Martín del Campo (eds.), *Diccionario
de Especialidades Farmacéuticas, Edición C.A.D.* (Mexico City: Ediciones
PLM, 5th ed., 1973).

6. Emilio Rosenstein and Alfonso Martín del Campo (eds.), *Diccionario
de Especialidades Farmacéuticas, Edición E. Co.* (Bogotá: PLM International, Colombia, 2nd ed., 1973).

7. Paulo B. de Carvalho Fontes (ed.), *Index Terapêutico Moderno* (São Paulo: Serviços de Publicações Especializadas, 2nd ed., 1973).

8. Juan E. Navarro Clarke and Juan A. Marrari (eds.), *Therapia Vademecum* (Buenos Aires: Therapia, 1973).

9. *Pills, Profits, and Politics,* p. 75.

10. U.S. Department of Health, Education, and Welfare, Office of the Secretary, Task Force on Prescription Drugs, *The Drug Prescribers* (Washington, D.C.: U.S. Government Printing Office, 1968), pp. 12, 50.

11. Ibid., pp. 12, 13.

12. Louis S. Goodman and Alfred Gilman (eds.), *The Pharmacological Basis of Therapeutics* (New York: Macmillan, 4th ed., 1970).

13. American Medical Association, Department of Drugs, *AMA Drug Evaluations* (Acton, Mass.: Publishing Sciences Group, 2nd ed., 1973).

2. *Antibiotics*

1. *Pills, Profits, and Politics,* p. 289.

2. Andrew W. Roberts and James A. Visconti, "The Rational and Irrational Use of Systemic Antimicrobial Drugs," *American Journal of Hospital Pharmacy* 29:1054 (October 1972).

3. Robert Maronde, cited in *Pills, Profits, and Politics,* p. 290.

4. Paul D. Stolley and Louis Lasagna, "Prescribing Patterns of Physicians," *Journal of Chronic Diseases* 22:395 (December 1969).

5. William R. McCabe, Bernard E. Kreger, and Margaret Johns, "Type-Specific and Cross-Reactive Antibodies in Gram-Negative Bacteremia," *New England Journal of Medicine* 287:261 (August 10, 1972).

6. Editorial, "Blood Dyscrasias Following the Use of Chloramphenicol," *Journal of the American Medical Association* 149:840 (June 28, 1952).

7. American Medical Association, Council on Pharmacy and Chemistry, *New and Nonofficial Remedies* (Philadelphia: Lippincott, 1953), p. 123.

8. American Medical Association, Council on Drugs, "Blood Dyscrasias Associated with Chloramphenicol (Chloromycetin) Therapy," *Journal of the American Medical Association* 172:2044 (April 30, 1960).

9. National Academy of Sciences/National Research Council, Panel on Anti-Infective Drugs (III), "Chloromycetin Solution," cited in U.S. Senate, Select Committee on Small Business, Subcommittee on Monopoly, *Effect of Promotion and Advertising of Over-the-Counter Drugs on Competition, Small Business, and the Health and Welfare of the Public* (Washington, D.C.: U.S. Government Printing Office) 3:1063-1072 (1972).

10. Henry Welch, C. N. Lewis, and I. Kerlan, "Blood Dyscrasias: A Nationwide Survey," *Antibiotics and Chemotherapy* 4:607 (June 1954).

11. Adrian Recinos, Jr., Sidney Ross, Bennett Olshaker, and Ellsworth Twible, "Chloromycetin in the Treatment of Pneumonia in Infants and Children: A Preliminary Report on Thirty-Three Cases," *New England Journal of Medicine* 241:733 (November 10, 1949).

12. William R. Best, "Chloramphenicol-Associated Blood Dyscrasias. A Review of Cases Admitted to the American Medical Association Registry," *Journal of the American Medical Association* 201:181 (July 17, 1967).

13. Harry F. Dowling, *Medicines for Man* (New York: Knopf, 1970), p. 279.

14. William Dameshek, statement in U.S. Senate, Select Committee on Small Business, Subcommittee on Monopoly, *Present Status of Competition in the Pharmaceutical Industry* (Washington, D.C.: U.S. Government Printing Office, 1968) 6:2390-2420.

15. American Medical Association, Council on Drugs, *AMA Drug Evaluations* (Chicago: American Medical Association, 1st ed., 1971), p. 387.

16. "La Administración de Alimentos y Medicamentos (E.U.A.) previene contra la prescripción excesiva de chloranfenicol," *Boletín de la Oficina Sanitaria Panamericana,* August 1968, p. 126.

17. World Health Organization, "Drug Information No. 95" (memorandum dated June 25, 1971).

18. Pan American Health Organization, memorandum dated May 10, 1972.

19. Michael Dunne, Andrew Herxheimer, Maynard Newman, and Helen Ridley, "Indications and Warnings About Chloramphenicol," *Lancet* 2:781 (October 6, 1973).

20. John F. Hellegers, "Chloramphenicol in Japan: Let It Bleed," *Bulletin of Concerned Asia Scholars* 5:37 (July 1973).

21. Maurice E. Shils, "Some Metabolic Aspects of Tetracyclines," *Clinical Pharmacology and Therapeutics* 3:321 (May-June 1962).

22. Goodman and Gilman, pp. 1259-1261.

23. Ibid., p. 1301.

24. Ibid., p. 1299.

25. *AMA Drug Evaluations,* p. 570.

26. Goodman and Gilman, p. 1298.

27. Floyd C. Russell et al. (eds.), *Vademecum Internacional de Especialidades Farmacéuticas y Biológicas, Edición COVPER* (Islamorada, Florida: J. Morgan Jones Publications, 18th ed., 1973), p. 15.

28. Jack S. Remington, Bradley Efron, Ellen Cavanaugh, Harold J. Simon, and Alfonso Trejos, "Studies on Toxoplasmosis in El Salvador. Prevalence and Incidence of Toxoplasmosis as Measured by the Sabin-Feldman Dye Test," *Transactions of the Royal Society of Tropical Medicine and Hygiene* 64:252-267 (April 1970).

3. *Oral Contraceptives*

1. *Pills, Profits, and Politics,* pp. 20, 98-103.

2. Ibid., pp. 100-102.

3. Royal College of General Practitioners, *Oral Contraceptives and Health* (Manchester, England: Pitman Medical, 1974).

4. Victor Cohn, "AMA Pledges All-Out Fight Against Birth-Pill Warning," *Washington Post,* June 24, 1970.

5. *AMA Drug Evaluations,* pp. 412, 413.

4. *Nonsteroid Antiarthritics*

1. Goodman and Gilman, p. 337.

2. Ibid., p. 335.

3. *AMA Drug Evaluations,* p. 298.

4. "Phenylbutazone and Oxyphenbutazone," *Medical Letter* 15 (No. 9):40 (April 27, 1973).

5. Ibid.

6. *AMA Drug Evaluations,* p. 298.

7. Goodman and Gilman, p. 337.

8. Robert F. Willkens and William M. O'Brien, "New Nonsteroidal Anti-Inflammatory Drugs (NSAID)" *Bulletin on the Rheumatic Diseases* 24:770 (1973-1974).

9. Goodman and Gilman, p. 337.

10. Ibid.

11. Donald Mainland (ed.), "A Three-Month Trial of Indomethacin in Rheumatoid Arthritis, with Special Reference to Analysis and Inference," *Clinical Pharmacology and Therapeutics* 8:11-37 (January-February 1967).

12. William M. O'Brien, "Indomethacin: A Survey of Clinical Trials," *Clinical Pharmacology and Therapeutics* 9:94-107 (January-February 1968).

13. Robert S. Pinals and Sumner Frank, "Relative Efficacy of Indomethacin and Acetylsalicylic Acid in Rheumatoid Arthritis," *New England Journal of Medicine* 276:512-514 (March 2, 1967).

14. Raymond Newberry, cited in U.S. Senate, Select Committee on Small Business, Subcommittee on Monopoly, *Present Status of Competition in the Pharmaceutical Industry* (Washington, D.C.: U.S. Government Printing Office, 1968) 7:2888.

15. Robert M. Hodges, statement, ibid., 7:2883-2892, 2895-2919.

16. Goodman and Gilman, p. 338.

17. Ibid.

5. *Steroid Hormones*

1. Goodman and Gilman, pp. 1631-1635.

2. Ibid., p. 1605.

3. *AMA Drug Evaluations,* pp. 387-389.

4. Boye J. Nielsen, Aa. Drivsholm, F. Fischer, and K. Brochner-Mortensen, "Long-Term Treatment with Corticosteroids in Rheumatoid Arthritis (Over a Period of 9 to 12 Years)," *Acta Medica Scandinavica* 173:177-183 (fasc. 2, 1963).

5. Hibbard E. Williams and Charles E. Becker, "Endocrine Disorders," in Kenneth L. Melmon and Howard F. Morrelli (eds.), *Clinical Pharmacology* (New York: Macmillan, 1972), p. 330.

6. David P. Lauler, Gordon H. Williams, and George W. Thorn, "Diseases of the Adrenal Cortex," in Maxwell M. Wintrobe et al. (eds.), *Harrison's Principles of Internal Medicine* (New York: McGraw-Hill, 6th ed., 1970), Vol. 1, p. 513.

7. *AMA Drug Evaluations,* pp. 382, 388.

8. Ibid., p. 382.

9. Ibid., p. 407.

10. Ibid., p. 403.

11. Goodman and Gilman, p. 1573.

12. Frederick H. Meyers, Ernest Jawetz, and Alan Goldfien, *Review of Medical Pharmacology* (Los Altos, Calif.: Lange Medical Publications, 2nd ed., 1970), pp. 369, 371.

13. *AMA Drug Evaluations,* p. 407.

6. *Antipsychotic Tranquilizers*

1. Goodman and Gilman, p. 155.

2. *AMA Drug Evaluations,* p. 325.

3. Ibid.

4. Ibid.

5. Goodman and Gilman, pp. 162, 165.

6. George E. Crane, "Tardive Dyskinesia in Patients Treated with Major Neuroleptics: A Review of the Literature," *American Journal of Psychiatry* (supp.) 124:40 (February 1968).

7. Arnold Bernstein and Henry L. Lennard, "Drugs Against People," *Society* 10:14 (May-June 1973).

8. P. F. Kennedy, H. I. Hershon, and R. J. McGuire, "Extrapyramidal Disorders After Prolonged Phenothiazine Therapy," *British Journal of*

Psychiatry 118:509-518 (May 1971).

9. Frank J. Ayd, "A Survey of Drug-Induced Extrapyramidal Reactions," *Journal of the American Medical Association* 175:1054 (March 25, 1961).

10. R. Degkwitz, W. Wenzel, K.-F. Binsack, H. Herkert, and O. Luxenburger, "Zum Problem der terminalen extrapyramidalen Hyperkinesen an Hand von 1600 langfristig mit Neuroleptica Behandelten," *Arzneimittel-Forschung* 16:276 (February 1966).

11. Daniel L. Greenblatt, Joan R. Dominick, Bernard A. Stotsky, and Alberto Di Mascio, "Phenothiazine-Induced Dyskinesia in Nursing-Home Patients," *Journal of the American Geriatric Society* 16:27 (January 1968).

12. William H. Anderson and John C. Kuehnle, "Strategies for the Treatment of Acute Psychosis," *Journal of the American Medical Association* 229:1884 (September 30, 1974).

13. H. I. Hershon, P. F. Kennedy, and R. J. McGuire, "Persistence of Extrapyramidal Disorders and Psychiatric Relapse After Withdrawal of Long-Term Phenothiazine Therapy," *British Journal of Psychiatry* 120:41-50 (January 1972).

7. *Antidepressants*

1. Goodman and Gilman, p. 181.
2. "Tofranil-PM and Antidepressant Therapy," *Medical Letter* 16 (No. 7):29 (March 29, 1974).
3. *AMA Drug Evaluations,* pp. 359, 360.
4. Leo E. Hollister, "Clinical Use of Psychotherapeutic Drugs: Current Status," *Clinical Pharmacology and Therapeutics* 10:170 (March-April 1969).
5. *AMA Drug Evaluations,* p. 361.
6. Ibid.
7. Ibid.
8. Ibid.
9. Goodman and Gilman, p. 185.
10. *AMA Drug Evaluations,* p. 360.
11. "Tofranil-PM and Antidepressant Therapy," *Medical Letter* 16 (No. 7):29 (March 29, 1974).

8. *Anticonvulsants*

1. Milton Silverman, *Magic in a Bottle* (New York: Macmillan, 2nd ed., 1948), p. 299.
2. Goodman and Gilman, p. 208.

3. *AMA Drug Evaluations,* p. 352.

4. Goodman and Gilman, pp. 210, 211.

5. *AMA Drug Evaluations,* pp. 348-350.

6. "Diphenylhydantoin," *Medical Letter* 13 (No. 12):50 (June 11, 1971).

7. Goodman and Gilman, p. 213.

8. Ibid.

9. *AMA Drug Evaluations,* p. 349.

10. Ibid., p. 353.

11. Ibid., p. 901.

12. Ibid.

13. Goodman and Gilman, p. 221.

14. *AMA Drug Evaluations,* p. 901.

9. *Discussion*

1. Michael Dunne, Andrew Herxheimer, Maynard Newman, and Helen Ridley, "Indications and Warnings About Chloramphenicol," *Lancet* 2:781 (October 6, 1973).

2. G. Teeling-Smith, "Ethics of Pharmaceutical Sales Promotion," in A. J. Jouhar and M. F. Grayson (eds.), *International Aspects of Drug Evaluation and Usage* (Edinburgh and London: Churchill Livingstone, 1973), p. 340.

3. Marcel Granier-Doyeux, "A Manero de Prologo," in Austra Spilva de Lehr, *Gúia de las Especialidades Farmacéuticas en Venezuela* (Madrid: Rivadeneyra, 1973).

4. Stuart K. Hensley, statement in *Annual Meeting Report 1972,* Warner-Lambert Company, New York, N.Y., May 2, 1972, pp. 5-7.

5. Personal communication, Mexico City, November 1974.

6. Richard J. Barnet and Ronald E. Müller, *Global Reach: The Power of the Multinational Corporations* (New York: Simon & Schuster, 1974).

7. Stuart K. Hensley, loc. cit.

8. *Codigo Sanitario de los Estados Unidos Mexicanos* (Mexico City: Secretaria de Salubridad y Asistencia, 1973), Article 275.

9. *Ley General de Salud* (San José, Costa Rica: Ministerio de Salud, 1974), Article 260.

10. *Leyes vigentes que regulan el ejercicio de la Profesión Farmacéutica, registro y venta de Medicamentos, etc., en la República de Nicaragua* (Managua: Inspeccion General de Farmacias, Ministerio de Salubridad Publica de Nicaragua, 1958), Chapter 7, Article 60.

11. "Metodos de Registro, Control y Venta de los Productos Farmacéuticos en el Area Centro America," in Francisco Alonso Martinez, *Prontuario del Quimico-Farmacéutico de El Salvador* (San Salvador: Colegio de Quimicos y

Farmacéuticos de El Salvador, 1969), p. 110.

12. "Reglamento de Especialidades Farmacéuticas," Chapter I, Article 19, ibid., p. 56.

13. *Codificación Sanitaria Nacional* (Bogotá: Ministerio de Salud Publica, 1967), Decree 1174, 1950, Article 6, p. 138.

14. Ibid., Resolution 000534, 1963, Article 3, p. 526.

15. Ibid., Decree 1289, 1964, Article 2, p. 364.

16. *Codigo de la Salud*, Ministerio de Salud Publica, Quito, May 10, 1971.

17. Serviço Naçional de Fiscalização da Medicina y Farmácia, Brasilia, Brasil, personal communication, 1975.

18. Barnet and Müller, *Global Reach*.

19. Personal communication, Mexico City, November 1974.

20. *Annual Survey Reports* (Washington, D.C.: Pharmaceutical Manufacturers Association).

21. Gaylord Nelson, statement in U.S. Senate, Select Committee on Small Business, Subcommittee on Monopoly, *Present Status of Competition in the Pharmaceutical Industry* (Washington, D.C.: U.S. Government Printing Office, 1967) 3:917.

22. Gaylord Nelson, ibid., 2:657.

23. Edmond M. Jacoby, Jr., and Dennis L. Hefner, "Domestic and Foreign Prescription Drug Prices," *Social Security Bulletin* 34:15 (May 1971).

24. *Pills, Profits, and Politics,* p. 180.

25. Barnet and Müller, *Global Reach,* p. 158.

26. Ibid., p. 16.

27. Personal communication, Mexico City, November 1974.

28. Personal communication, Bogotá, December 1974.

29. Personal communication, Bogotá, December 1974.

30. Jean L. Whitehill, managing editor, *Carta Medica*, personal communication, 1975.

31. Michael Dunne et al., "Indications," ibid.

32. Zoheir Farid, Walter F. Miner, Anwar Hassan, and Bishara Trabolsi, "Misuse of Antibiotics," *New England Journal of Medicine* 292:216 (January 23, 1975).

33. Silvia Aladjem, "Chloramphenicol in South America," *New England Journal of Medicine* 281:1369 (December 11, 1969).

34. Hernando Sarasti, "Chloramphenicol in South America (Cont.)," *New England Journal of Medicine* 282:813 (April 2, 1970).

35. Jacobo Ghitis, "Chloramphenicol in South America (Cont.)," *New England Journal of Medicine* 282:813 (April 2, 1970).

36. L. Sánchez Medal, J. P. Castanedo, and F. García Rojas, "Insecticides and Aplastic Anemia," *New England Journal of Medicine* 269:1365 (December 19, 1963).

37. Luis Sánchez Medal and Samuel Dorantes, "Aplastic Anemia," *Paediatrician* 3:74 (1974).

38. G. Teeling-Smith in Jouhar and Grayson, op. cit., p. 337.

39. *Pills, Profits, and Politics,* pp. 89-94.

40. Ibid., pp. 64, 65.

41. Bentley Glass, *Science and Ethical Values* (Chapel Hill: University of North Carolina Press, 1965).

42. Bentley Glass, "The Ethical Basis of Science," *Science* 150:1254 (December 3, 1965).

43. Van R. Potter, "Bioethics for Whom?" *Annals of New York Academy of Sciences* 196:200 (June 7, 1972).

INDEX

Achromycin and Acromicina, 7, 16-18
Acromax, 11
Acromaxfenicol, 11
Advertising. *See* Promotion, drug
American Medical Association, 8-9, 24; *AMA Drug Evaluations,* 5, 24-25, 34
American Rheumatism Association, 35
Amfostat. *See* Fungizone
Amphotericin B, 7, 10, 12, 19-20
Ampliactil and Amplictil, 61, 65-68
Anderson, W., 62-63
Anfertil. *See* Ovral
Antiarthritics, nonsteroid, 33-48
Antibiotics, 7-22. *See also* individual drugs by generic or brand name
Anticonvulsants, 93-105
Antidepressants, 76-92. *See also* MAO inhibitors and Tricyclic antidepressants
Aplastic anemia, 11, 94, 97, 127-128
Aristocort and Ledercort, 49, 52, 54-58
Avantyl and Aventyl, 76, 79, 88-89, 131
Ayd, F., 62

Barnet, R., and Müller, R., 116, 120
Bejarano, A., 114
Betamethasone, 49, 52, 54-58
Blood dyscrasias, 8, 11, 97
Boehringer, 7, 11, 13-15
Bromides, 93
Brujo. See Witch doctor
Butazolidin and Butazolidina, 33, 36, 38-41

Calvo Nuñez, H., 116
Carbamazepine, 93-97, 103-105
Carta Medica, 123, 124
Celestone, 49, 52, 54-58
Charpentier, P., 61

Children and drug use, 35, 51-52, 53, 64, 77, 78, 79, 96
Chloramphenicol, 2, 7, 8-9, 10-11, 13-15, 107, 109, 126-128
Chloromycetin, 7, 9, 11, 13-15
Chlorpromazine, 61-68
Ciba-Geigy, 33, 36-37, 38-41, 42-45, 93, 103-105, 119. *See also* Geigy
Cloramfenicol MK and Cloranfenicol MK, 7, 11, 13-15
Cloranfenicol "Cloranficina," 7, 11, 13-15
Contraceptives, oral, 23-32, 117-118
Corticosteroid hormones, 49-50, 51-58
Courvoisier, S., 61

Depression, 76, 78-80
Desipramine, 76, 79, 85-87
Detail men, 110, 112, 121-124. *See also* Drug companies and Promotion, drug
Difenil Hidantoinata MK. *See* Kessodanten
Dilantin and Epamin, 93, 95-96, 98-100
Diphenylhydantoin, 93, 94, 95, 98-100
Disclosure, 106, 108-109. *See also* Food and Drug Administration and Promotion, drug
Drug companies: ethics, xii, 108-113, 128-133; multinationality, 111, 112-113, 116, 117, 131-132; profits, 112-113, 119-120, 121. *See also* Detail men and Promotion, drug
Drugs. *See* Laws, drug; Prescription of drugs; and Prices of drugs
Dunne, M., 9, 126
Dyskinesia, tardive, 62-64

Epamin. *See* Dilantin
Epilepsy, 93-105

JI

RM301 .S53   c.1
Silverman, Milton Mo   100107 000
The drugging of the Americas :

3 9310 00032658 5
GOSHEN COLLEGE-GOOD LIBRARY